BARNEY FIFE'S
Guide *to* Life
LOVe *and*
Self-Defense

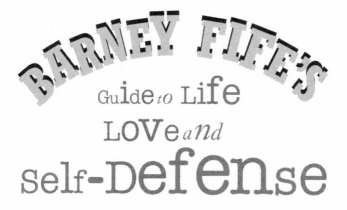

BARNEY FIFE'S
Guide *to* Life
LOVE *and*
Self-Defense

with Len and John Oszustowicz

THE SUMMIT GROUP

FORT WORTH, TEXAS

THE   SUMMIT   GROUP

1227 West Magnolia, Suite 500, Fort Worth, Texas, 76104
*Published 1993. Printed in the United States of America.
Design by Cheryl Corbitt.*

10   9   8   7   6   5   4   3   2   1

*Photos on pages 4, 11, 16, and 96 are courtesy of
the* Tennessean *and the* Nashville Banner.

Oszustowicz, Len and John:
*Barney Fife's guide to life, love and self-defense/Len and John
Oszustowicz.*

p. cm.
Includes black and white photographs
ISBN 1-56530-103-X

*1. Humor. 2. Self-help. 3. The Andy Griffith Show.
4. Mayberry RFD. 5. Don Knotts. 6. U.S. deputies.
7. Television comedies. I. Oszustowicz, Len and John. II. Title.*

For our dad,
Leonard Andrew Oszustowicz,
a man of character
and kindness
who would be right at home
in Mayberry

All author's royalties from the
sale of this book will be donated to the
following charities:
Make A Wish Foundation
A Wish With Wings
Dedicated to granting wishes for children
with life-threatening diseases

coNtents

~~~~~~~~~~

~~~~~~~~~~

1

How It All Got Started

The icy blood of a crimefighter
courses through my veins — my being cannot
rest while evil lurks. . . .

Police work is in my blood and denying that would be a waste of time. I was born to defend the little man and ever since I was young that's all I ever really dreamed of doing. "Like an animal drawn to water" — that's what Ma said when I told her that I was going to make keeping the peace my life's work. I knew from the start that I was called to serve, but I was never sure which direction my career would take. I considered the FBI, but since I was born and bred right here in Mayberry, it seemed clear that I would end up back home.

So here I am in Mayberry. Mayberry's a fine town, ya' know. The folks are real nice and the weather's about as good as you'll find anywhere.

"I don't care if this car belongs to the Governor himself. He's gone and bought himself a traffic ticket compliments of Barney Fife."

But the real thing that made me decide to stay in Mayberry was that Andy really needed me. It was just too much for any one man to fight off the beasts of prey that come down out of the forest and threaten the good citizens of Mayberry. So the Sheriff needed help, and after carefully reviewing the candidates, cousin Andy chose me. And I answered the call to serve. Since that day, Mayberry has been a safer place to live, and I've been a man with a purpose — to defend the weak against those who would take advantage.

My many years on the Force have taught me to watch, listen, and learn. That's the difference between a lawman and a civilian — a lawman's always taking it all in, even when he looks like he's just sitting around. On the other hand, when you see a civilian sitting around it's probably just some county employee goldbricking again. Anyhow, I've taken advantage of my years in upholding the law to learn a lot about people, and why and how they do things. From time to time I've even given my opinion on what I think of this or that. And folks seemed to be interested.

Then it hit me! I said to myself, "Hey, Barn, why not put your thoughts in a book? Sure, that's

"The most important thing about my firearm is safety."

Gomer

Thelma Lou

➤

**"You're a regular
Felix the Cat, you
are."**

it! Crank up the old pen-ola and let 'er
rip. That way, everybody could learn from my experience. I could write about protecting folks, and
where to find good food, and what to wear and, of
course, finding yourself the right girl."

N ow, as you know, I'm not one who likes to
talk about himself. But it did strike me that a
book might be the way to go.

So I talked to Thelma Lou and she told
me that she thought that any book I'd write
would be "very interesting." Gomer said
that he thought that it would sell at least
as well as *The Beast That Ate Boston.*

Floyd said, "Yes . . . yes . . . Barney
writing a book. Could be interesting. A

Floyd

Aunt Bee

little like the memoirs of Calvin Coolidge, I suppose. Insightful . . . and fun!" Aunt Bee thought that I should think carefully about such a large undertaking, but not on an empty stomach. The last person I asked was Andy. He said, "To put it in your own words, Barn, it would be big. Really big. The biggest thing to happen in these parts for a long time."

"Most criminal types can be helped by constructive hobbies such as woodcarving and Mr. Potato Head Sets."

So, taking the advice of my very best friends and relying in part on Fife instinct, I decided to give it a go. So here it is. *Barney Fife's Guide to Life, Love and Self-Defense.*

Now, some of my advice is real simple. I explain why you should

Andy

stop dating a girl if her mother's still tagging along after more than a month. That advice is pretty simple, but real important nonetheless. Other areas of my advice are more serious, like some good rules for bringing up kids and some basic philosophies of how to treat others.

Whether simple or a little more serious, everything I say in this book I learned from the people of Mayberry. They've sure taught me a few lessons through the years, and I'd just like to pass them on to you, whether you're from Mount Pilot or Philadelphia or any place in between.

So, without spouting off any further, here are my thoughts on a few things and a short summary of how the world looks through the eyes of Barney Fife — America's Deputy (Kinda catchy, ain't it?).

"You knoW how I feel about fuss and falderol. Lord knows the job itself is reward enough."

2

Courtin'

(Or Datin', if You Live North of Richmond)

Ne'er was the woman born
whose heart could resist a uniform. . . .

There we were — *sitting in the last row of the theater watching Cary Grant cast his spell. Out of the corner of my eye I see Thelma Lou gazing with longing eyes — first at me, then at the screen. Then back at me, and then back again at the screen. Then she smiled at me . . . and sighed.*

"You know what I'm going to do? I'm going to go home, change, drop by Thelma Lou's and watch that George Raft movie on T-V."

A Fife is a Fife is a Fife. Ya' just can't deny genes. The bold nose, the strong chin, and the deep-set eyes conjure their magic with the women. But even in spite of the physical gifts I was given, there are many things I had to learn about courting (or dating, if you prefer). Hard to believe as it is, though, even I've made some mistakes and learned from 'em. I hope that by explaining what I've learned I can help you find a shortcut on the road to *amor.*

Now, be honest with yourself for a second. You and I both know that the reason you bought my book was to see what tips you could pick up from ol' Barn on romance. Right? So I decided to put this chapter right up here in the front. That way, you can use it as a kind of reference book, and it'll be real convenient to get to.

O f course, my dating experience may not relate to the common man. A lot of my perspectives on courting are clouded by where I've been and what I've done. Having been Mayberry's most-eligible bachelor two of the last five years at the reunion makes it hard for me to be objective. (Andy won twice and Goober once.) And don't think for a second that just because I've limited myself to Thelma Lou for so many years that I've lost my feel for the heat of the Mayberry scene. Love is alive and well in Mayberry, and the temperature's rising!

"Marry in haste. . . repent in leisure."

In any event, here are a few rules to pave your road to romance with cobblestones of experience from one that knows what he's saying. When the ladies refer to "Tweeky," "Barney-Parney-Poo," and "Cream Puff," they ain't talking about their ironing boards, ya' know.

Rule number one — *numero uno* — is to only date a girl who likes to eat the same kind of things you like. Just in case your courting turns serious, you've got to think ahead. Say, for example, that you like your pizza pie with pepperelli and you're seeing somebody who doesn't like nothing but mozzarella. There ya' are, setting yourself up for a lifetime of picking off pepperellis. Picking off pepperellis leads to bickering about how the mozzarella slices still taste like pepperelli even after ya' take 'em off. Next thing ya' know you're squabbling and pretty soon — *kablooey!* The whole deal's off. Nope, find out what she eats before you ask her out.

"A man of action can't be worried about how his hair is combed."

I'll Have the
Blue Plate Special, Please

Now, if you must ask a girl out without knowing about her eating habits, the first date should always be to go out to eat. Now, say ya' go to the Bluebird Diner and they have a blue plate special along with their regular-priced menu. Now, even though it's Dutch, pay real close attention here. If she picks the blue plate, that's good. Why pay an extra dime for a meal that's no better than the special? If she orders off the regular menu you'll know she doesn't understand the value of a dollar. A lesson better learned on the first date than later.

It just defies explanation . . . but there's something about a Fife that just sets women off.

On Your Mark. . .
Now, after she's ordered, watch to see how fast she eats. If she sets onto her food like Otis to a fresh jug, look out. You'll find yourself in a life-long battle, and more than likely you'll end up with the necks and gizzards while she's eating white meat.

"Our only crime is that we're attractive to women."

We Won't Even Have to Wash the Dishes
Mama Fife always had a rule that we were to clean our plates before we left the table. Waste not, want not. But that was never a problem because us Fifes have always been big eaters. But remember that the purpose of your courting is to find yourself a steady girl. You're not looking for somebody to run a team of mules. So watch your date. If she was raised properly, she'll eat a fair amount and then stop. That's a

good sign. If she takes the plate down to the varnish and then goes at it with a heel of bread to sop up what's left, you've got a problem. She'll eat you out of house and home — and a dollar a week extra on the food bill will add up.

Now, I could go on and on about the importance of this first point, but I think you're getting the idea. You can learn a lot about a person from watching her at meal time. And remember — if you end up marrying this girl you're going to spend more time eating with her than any other thing. If you were to marry her and stay married for fifty years, you'd spend more than five of those years across the table from one another. That's something to keep in mind! So get off on the right foot and get a read on how she eats.

Dealing With Mothers

The second rule is to quit taking her mother along on dates after the first month or so. Now, it's perfectly reasonable for a lady's mother to come along on the first few dates. That's just a custom of polite society. But if after a month or so your date keeps dragging her mother along, you've got a problem (not to mention an awful waste of money for

"It's her own fault. Who ever told her to fall in love with me?"

12

the extra popcorn). So, if after a few weeks Ma keeps showing up, take it from me: Nip it! Nip it! Nip it!

The trick is to watch and see if your date gets rid of the extra baggage or if she doesn't make any such move. If she leaves it up to you to get rid of her mother, she simply doesn't understand romance. And that sure won't do.

A Fallback Position

Another rule is to only date someone you like. Now, to the layman this seems obvious. But that just goes to prove how little you really know about the subject of love. There's so little time and so many women! Date only girls who, if things don't work out, will understand and remain your friend. It just doesn't do for a bachelor to have his reputation stained by those who have loved . . . and lost.

"Don't mess with Foxy Fife."

Serenade Your Sweetie

Over the years I've learned that a woman just can't resist a fella that sings to her. Now, once again I realize that everybody wasn't blessed with Fife vocal chords. Sometimes when I sing, my voice comes surging out of my body like Niagara Falls coming over that cliff in Rochester, New York. It's just sonic. But even if your voice is only average, try serenading your girl. She'll love it!

You might even try writing your girl a special song. I wrote Juanita a song once:

> *Juanita, Juanita,*
> *Lovely, dear Juanita,*
> *From your head down to your feet,*
> *There's nothing half so sweet,*
> *As Juanita, Juanita, Juanit.*
>
> *Oh, there are things of wonder,*
> *Of which men like to sing.*
> *There are pretty sunsets and birds upon the wing,*
> *But of the joys of nature,*
> *None truly can compare,*
> *With Juanita, Juanita, she of beauty beyond*
> *   compare.*
> *Juanita, Juanita, lovely dear Juanit.*

"My voice teacher **(Eleanora Poultice)** claims that **my voice is out of this world."**

Need I say more?

Love Letters

Now, it appears to me that most fellas miss the boat when it comes to letter writing, too. Take it from ol' Barn that the way to a woman's heart is through her reading glasses. There ain't a woman alive that wouldn't kill to get a love letter from her fella. Ya' know — the kind of letter that's swimming in bay rum — smells like a new haircut. And you know how the ladies go for a man with a new haircut! (I believe that's the very reason why Floyd Lawson has been able to build his empire in Mayberry. He's not cutting hair — he's selling an amperdesiac. It just makes women crazy, which, of course, is why I get my hair cut each and every third Monday of the month.)

Anyway, I figure that men don't write very many love letters because they don't want to be thought of as mushy and sensitive. Of course, us Fifes are all sensitive, and it's never caused anybody to think of us as weak folks. Sensitive is sensitive and weak is weak. But sensitive ain't weak. Us Fifes are sensitive. But weak? Never in a million years!

The question I ask you is this: Would you rather be thought of as rough and tough and sit home every Saturday night, or would you rather be thought of as sweet and sensitive and be out sparking? Of course, I've been lucky to have my cake and eat it, too, when it comes to tough and sensitive all

"Goober'll **horn right in** at the dance tonight dragging that **albatross with him.**"

"He buttered **her up** and she **egged him on.**"

Poor Thel, sometimes she just can't help herself.

rolled into one ball. Trust ol' Barn. Write a love letter and then practice your puckering. It works every time. It just drives 'em wild.

The Standard Form Love Letter

Now then, what should a fella say in a letter to his girl? What can you say that will make her fall for you all over again? First, it's real important that you call her by her right name. This is a trick sometimes, especially if a fella works up a real good letter and uses it with several different girls. I learned this lesson the hard way one time when I sent Juanita a letter that my cousin Virgil had recommended. In the excitement I forgot to change the name and I sent Juanita a letter addressed to:

"Darling Ethel, Lilac of My Life"

Juanita didn't speak to me for a long time after I sent that letter. It took me two weeks to convince her that it was just a typographical error. I'm not sure she ever really bought the story, leading me to believe that there might be some of this same kind of letter recycling going on among the *ladies* of Mayberry, too. (This sounds a lot like a 266: violating the copyright of somebody else's written work. What kind of person would have anything to do with copying a love letter anyway? A real loser, that's who. Love letters are serious, personal things. What kind'a guy passes these things around? I just can't figure what the earth's coming to. Folks ought to be ashamed of themselves.)

If you do decide like I did, however, that a love letter with a track record is better than anything you can come up with on your own, let me suggest one that's worked for me many times:

(write the date here)

My Darling _____,

How many times each day do I think of you? Ten? Eleven? Twelve? I could never count how much I think of you, _____. When I brush my teeth, it's you I see in the mirror! When I eat my oatmeal, it's your face I see in the bowl! When I shine my shoes, you're right there on the toe. It's you, it's you, it's you, sweet _____.

"Dogs is dogs and people is people; one sticks his nose in a woodchuck hole and one don't. One you'd kiss on the mouth and the other you wouldn't."

"**A man does** with what he's got."

But without you, there is no sun, no joy. Like making ice cream with weak rock salt, my life without you is runny and cold — a time of sorrow. I count the minutes until we are together again and beg that heaven will allow us to run into each other somewhere today.

I can't live without you! My heart longs to be near your heart, my hands in your hands and my lips nibbling on the lobe of your ear. But until I'm with you, have a good thought of me and be patient — your Barn is near!

xxxoooxxx,

Barney

That one does the trick every time. It's the rich metaphor tied in with the pointed personal references. Smooth as Aunt Bee's banana cream pie.

While I'm at it, a second thing you will want to remember is to not send the same letter to the same girl more than once a year or so. If you're really in a fix, maybe you can even get away with it every nine months. Hopefully, she'll forget what you said before and you'll be able to get three or four runs on any letter you write. If you use the same "hot" letter more than that, though, you might give the impression that you're not sincere.

Finally, I ask you: On what occasions should a fella send his girl a love letter? Holidays? Birthdays? Before big dates? After big dates? When she's sick in bed? You tell me. Well, I'll tell ya' this much. The more you write, the more she'll pucker. So if you want all that sugar to go to waste, read your books and bait your line. If you want sweet romance, get out a good pencil and go to it.

"Why don't we go up to the hospital some night and take the bolts out of the wheel-chairs? That'd be funny, too."

The Best Dates

After you've done your studying on a girl's eating and you've wooed her with letters and singing and you've gotten rid of her mother, then it's time for regular courting. Here are a few kinds of dates that have been good for me. You might want to try a few out.

"I saw an Italian movie 'BREAD, LOVE AND BEANS' that was plenty risque."

Rock skipping out at Hopkins' Lake. This date combines two of the most important things a date's got to be. Number one, private. And number two, reasonably priced. For the price of a couple of bottles of pop at Wally's Filling Station on the way, you can have a full day of fun and privacy. The rocks are free (ha ha).

A picnic lunch out near the Robert E. Lee Natural Bridge.
You can never go wrong on a picnic since it can be
very private and, if you play your cards right, your
girl will bring the picnic lunch. (You can supply
the java — it's only fair to share the cost.)

Playing car bingo (not for money) *on the front porch.*
You wouldn't believe the number of different kinds
of cars two people can count in a couple of hours.
The only problem is that I just can't relax watching
'em speed by at twenty-five or thirty miles an hour.
Barney Fife may be on a date, but Deputy Fife stays
on duty.

Driving to Sanford (Brick Capital of the World —
it says so right there on the sign as you go into town)
and touring the brick factory (free admission *and* they'll
give each of you a real brick to keep as a souvenir).
This is a little on the technical side, so you should
only try this with a girl who's broad-minded enough
to be interested in this sort of futuristic thing.

And for those special spring days when the air's
cool and the pine smell is real pretty in the air, *go to the
regional airport in Raleigh and watch the planes come in from
Greensboro and Winston-Salem,* and practically anywhere
else in the state. The first one to see the beacon light
at the airport gets an extra scoop of ice cream at the

"You don't just come out and **kiss a deputy** sheriff on the **jaw right on the street.**"

I'd say that the Mayberry Police Force has done all right for itself, wouldn't you?

commissary that's right there in the terminal.

If you make it through this list of dates and are still getting on well with the girl, then ol' Barn has steered ya' right. You're on your own from here out, but remember: You're not home free yet. As ya' con-

"You know what they say about a man who keeps putting off marriage ... he gets irritable."

tinue to court her, think like a Fife! You've been taught by the master, now think like the master. When in doubt, ask yourself, "What would Barney do in this situation?" That's all you'll ever need to remember.

"It's a jungle out there, and I've got to hunt 'em down."

3

Law Enforcement

*Enforcement of the laws is the
keystone of every great civilization . . .*

Here lies Bernard P. Fife: Lawman, Citizen and Friend. That's how I hope the people of Mayberry will remember me one day. I take the law game seriously because it's the root of the American system. Every American is guaranteed life, liberty and the pursuit of happiness — it's right there in the National Anthem. But not one in ten folks realizes that it's us lawmen pounding the beat that makes those guarantees mean something. I'm the second-ranking lawman in the town of Mayberry, and I'm mighty proud of it.

Law enforcement is a rewarding profession. A body gets a lot of satisfaction in knowing that he is the first line of defense against those who would take advantage of others. But believe you me, law

"I'll have that crook off the street in 24 hours or my name's not 'Reliable Barney Fife'."

enforcement can get ugly. You try tangling with the likes of some of the criminal types that come by here in an average week, not to mention nuts like Ernest T. Bass. I've seen all kinds here in Mayberry, from counterfeiters to moonshiners to con men to pickpockets to gamblers. Each is dangerous in his own way.

It's a wilderness out there. And every so often a beast of prey comes sneaking in. Now, it's my job as a lawman to stalk him and run him out. That's my number one job — stalking, not fly-killing. It's a dirty job, but it's got to be done. And since it's got to be done, I'll give my level best to see that it's done right.

"Suppose he's a bathtub murderer? The ones that act simple and nice are your true schizophreeniacs."

Now, from time to time I've been accused of holding to the letter of the law a little too tight, especially when it comes to jaywalking, parking near hydrants, the speed limit and the like. But as I always say, "Give a man an inch and he'll take a mile; give him forty miles an hour and he'll take forty-five." Well, so long as Bernard P. Fife is wearing this badge, not so much as an inch will be given. You got to get up pretty early in the morning to put one past Eagle Eye Fife. Pretty early indeed.

Now, because many of you are reading this book to learn some of the finer points of law enforcement, I'm obliged to address a few key angles of the law business. Remember — many of these things we're going to discuss are meant for trained lawmen and are not to be trifled with by John Q. Citizen. So, be careful!

Are Deputies Really Necessary?

Upholding the law is a twenty-four-hour-a-day, seven-day-a-week, fifty-two-week-a-year job. It goes with the territory. Sure, it'd be convenient if the troublemakers would make an appointment, but most ain't quite that cooperative. And even if they were, the job's just too big for any one man. Even if that man's name is Andy Taylor. A qualified deputy is fully capable of filling in, whether the Sheriff just has to run over to Raleigh or if a crisis erupts and he's injured in the line of duty.

From time to time there'll be talk up in Raleigh about tightening the purse strings of government and cutting back on deputies. Some G-man sits at his desk in the capitol, doing his calculations while outside in the hall a policeman stands guard. I guess it's a compliment when folks take you so

> **"Knitters and crocheters seldom have stomach disorders."**

much for granted that they even forget the reason you're there in the first place. But look-e-see what happens when there's a ruckus and one of those politicians gets hurt. They'll start giving speeches and promising to spend whatever it takes to assure folks of their safety.

Are deputies important? They sure enough are.

The Importance of a Uniform

What does a uniform mean to you? Authority? Safety? Efficiency? A friend? Probably all of these things and more. You see, a uniform makes a statement. It says, "The man wearing this uniform stands for something." Many of our moms taught us at a young age that if you get in trouble, find a person in a uniform. What higher compliment could a mother pay to a man than to trust her young 'un to him?

Those wearing uniforms should try to live up to the high responsibilities they take on when they wear one. A uniform should be worn with pride and should always be cleaned, starched and pressed. The long and short of it is that a uniform isn't just clothes — it's a badge of honor.

The regulations clearly state the do's and don'ts of a uniform, and I could rattle 'em off line and

"I'm a student of humanity. I guess that's the difference between a sharply honed lawman and a jerk wearin' a badge."

Under Hat —
Regulation Book

Regulation Hat
(Complies With Section
215-23(a).)
Never Been On
Anyone Else's Head

The Importance of a Uniform

Standard Regulation
Neckwear

100% Cotton,
Genuine Whiplash
Cord Uniform

Regulation Patch
Identifying You
as One of
The Good Guys

The Badge of
Honor

Section 23
Approved
Accessory to
Neckwear (See
Chapter 7,
Page 90)

Bullet

Hidden behind
my arm "Old Roscoe"

Double Cuff Buttons
Assure Sleeve Will Not
Bind in the Event of a
Quick Draw

verse (and you know I could). But if a man needs
regulations to tell him what he can and can't do while
in uniform, he's probably not the kind who should
be wearing it in the first place.

Of course, none of this holds if your name is
Ernest T. Bass. Can you believe that I had to give that
nut my 100 percent cotton, genuine whiplash cord
uniform just so that he could show off for the girls?
That man was just dying to have a uniform like Jailsick
Sturman's so that he could find sweet romance. Sweet
romance, my foot! That guy's a nut — a nut running
around in *my best uniform!*

"I'll give it to you straight from the buttonhole. This bank is a crackerbox and a pushover. I cannot see one counter-measure in the event of a '10-12'."

The Squad Car

Hannibal had his elephants. Patton had his
tanks. Fife has his squad car. That's the way
I see it. The job of enforcing the law can be made
much easier if modern anticrime equipment can
be put into play. Our squad car bears the most up-
to-date crime detection equipment that's available
on the market. Although it is a multipurpose vehicle (used to carry groceries to widows and rakes
to the baseball field), we keep it in a constant state
of readiness. The light and siren were even specially ordered to fit perfectly on top of the black

**"Nip it!
Nip it!
Nip it!
Nip it in the bud."**

and white. One of the few differences Andy and me have when it comes to crimefighting is how much modern technology should be used. I'm a hardware man. Andy's not. Ya' either are or ya' ain't. Andy ain't. I am.

I believe that a man who takes his life in his hands on a daily basis should use all of the newest tools to tip the odds in his favor. Take vehicles, for example. With only one squad car we can't properly respond to a 328 (two incidents taking place at the same time). Say one fella dropped his car in a ditch over by Harnett and at the same time another blows through town at thirty miles an hour. As it is now, you've gotta make a decision whether to cover the 413 or the 270. You simply can't do both with one vehicle. Modern law enforcement has just passed by the one-patrol-car department — left it like an extinct animal lying dead alongside the highway of life.

For that very reason, I tried to place another vehicle into service. You remember the motorcycle I got so cheap over at the army surplus auction? It would've hit the nail right on the head. *El perfecto* answer. Two emergencies, two vehicles. It ain't brain surgery, for heaven's sake. Too bad that old mo-

> **"Who died and left you the boss? Why don't you go sit in the grocery store so we'll all know you're the big cheese."**

torcycle had such a historic past and had to be put in a museum. It would'a fit the bill just fine.

➡ **"Don't wear my hat. I can't stand to wear a hat when it's been on somebody else's head."**

Surveillance and Stakeouts

A trained lawman learns early that the party with the element of surprise on his side has got the advantage. That's the reason surveillance by law enforcement officials is critical. We've gotta get the jump on them before they get the jump on us. Besides, it kind'a ruins the effect if the fella being surveilled knows somebody's watching him.

Ben Weaver's store would be an empty shell by now if it wasn't for surveillance. After some hard thinking on the subject, I believe that I can offer some advice on the subject that might be useful one day to those of you considering the police game. Let me tell ya' about 'em.

Food and Drink: Take along plenty of food and drink. Now, in deciding the kinds of food to take, you should avoid anything that might tip the other fella off that you're around. Tuna fish is real bad because if the smell doesn't give you away, the cats will. Another loser is anything that's gas producing or fusses with your system, like pepperelli or salami or snap beans. You figure it out.

Along these same lines let me just mention in passing that personal grooming comes into the picture, too. Specifically, after-shave lotions and toilet water like Paris Nights might be OK for a night out on the town, but it sure doesn't work for a stakeout. That is, unless you're staking out a paint factory.

As far as beverages go, remember that most stakeouts ain't carried out in restrooms. For this reason, you've got to take it easy when it comes to drinking. One time I lost contact with a suspect in a 402 because I had to duck around behind the bushes. If you think I got in trouble for losing the suspect you don't know the half of it. Compared to the chewing I took from Mrs. Cruteck, what Andy said was nothing. Ya' see, the bushes I went around behind were Mrs. Cruteck's prize Forsythia. At least they *were!* Lesson learned.

An Alert Mind: Take along plenty to read. All the while you're keeping tabs on the suspect, it's good that you provide yourself some entertainment to help pass the time and keep your mind sharp. Since Andy doesn't let me take Thelma Lou with me anymore, I favor reading a good book or writing a letter to my cousin Virgil or somebody else I miss.

➡ **"Sure is good to be doing a capacity business. Both cells filled up."**

My favorite stakeout book is *The Oddesy* by a fella named Homer. I don't recall his last name. (It's a book about old-time Greece — come to think of it, it might be about some of Lydia Crosswaithe's kinfolk. They were from ancient Greece, ya' know. Nice gal, that Lydia. I've always felt bad about calling her an albatross over at Andy's that one time.)

If a serious book is too much for me some nights, I might thumb through the most recent issue of *Manhunt* magazine to make sure that I'm using the most up-to-date techniques in the law.

Some folks say that reading on stakeouts is boring, but to me it's stimulating. That's why I do it. It keeps my mind sharp. And a stakeout without a sharp mind is like a comb without teeth — just a waste of time.

"Now look alive! Snap to! This is a jail."

Be Inconspicuous (Don't Stick Out): Think like an animal melting into the shadows. This is harder for some of us than for others because some of us just naturally stand out in a crowd. Take me, for instance. I don't know how many times I've heard folks tell me that they could pick me out of a crowd as being a lawman (though many mistake me for the Sheriff or the Mayor). I guess the position sounds

A properly trained Lawman like me can melt into the background. Can you tell which one is me?

important, so folks go looking for an important-looking man. So it's tougher for me than most. It's the distinctive Fife features that make it tough. The strong chin, the deep-set mysterious eyes, the prominent cheekbones, the chiseled figure (no fat, all muscle). These are features that make me stand out. So I have to try extra hard to blend in. To do that, I use a lot of disguises, and I'll talk about them later.

Finally, you should look disinterested. This to me is just like acting out a part. Of course, over the years I've played big roles in many a production around Mayberry (Noogatuck in Mayberry's Founder's Day Pageant and a featured part in *Rose Marie*, to name but two). Ask any

"I thought maybe I'd drop old J. Edgar a note. . . just to feel him out."

actor and they'll tell you that the key to acting is to find a role model. That's a show biz term that means ya' find somebody who acts like the character you're playing and then you study him. Then you act your part just like you learned from the person you watched.

Well, when it comes to looking disinterested I think there is no better role model than Goober Pyle. That's why I spend so much time hanging around Wally's Filling Station. Most folks probably think I'm goldbricking when I'm out there drinking a root beer. Goes to show ya' what civilians know — I'm studying my role model.

Webster's Dictionary defines Disinterested as "Not having the mind or feelings engaged."

Record Keeping: Take good notes. This is always a big part of proper police procedure, but when on a stakeout it is specially important. When taking notes at a stakeout scene, it's necessary to log the time, suspected perpetrator's movements (what the guy that you're watching is doing), and any comings or goings in the general area that you're staking out. These should be logged into a standard

"You know how Floyd is. He can't move his jaws and scissors at the same time."

Department of Public Safety Log Book (State Law Enforcement Equipment Catalog number 3445-89) so that the pages you fill out will fit into the Master Log Book (catalog number 3445-89A) that is maintained at all times on the shelf next to Opie's stamp collection.

There is one potential problem that you must be aware of in keeping notes on stakeouts. Be careful that the notes you're taking on the stakeout don't get mixed up with the other writing you're doing. One time I got crossed up and I sent Juanita a stakeout report and I sent the North Carolina State Police in Raleigh a four-page love letter (in triplicate). *El big problemo.* Could'a turned out worse — Juanita was real impressed at how important my work is and I got a return letter from a secretary that works up at the State Police Headquarters. That Fife magic even works through the U.S. mail!

Disguise: Above I discussed the challenge of looking common when you're not. Clothes can be used to draw attention even from the most handsome face. Over the years I've used dresses, hunting clothes and lots of other outfits to try to keep attention away from myself. Remember — the more normal

"Well, friends, as Mr. Lawson told you, I'm Deputy Sheriff Barney Fife; although I have a nickname I've been stuck with and can't seem to lose: 'Fast Gun Fife.' "

you can look, the better. For this reason, for example, if I were going to have to dress up like an old lady (I just hate that) to break up a bookmaking racket down at Floyd's, I would select a printed floral over a geometric. The floral would allow me to blend in with the other women of Mayberry while a geometric would call too much attention to my physique. Ya' just can't hide the Fife physique. It's just too noticeable — man or woman, young or old, a Fife's a Fife.

A man's gotta do what a man's gotta do.

Hot Pursuit

You're now talking about the most dangerous part of the law enforcement game. I've placed this topic way down deep in this chapter so that no young 'uns would leaf through and come upon this topic by mistake. This is life-and-death stuff, but then again, danger just comes with the territory.

There's two reasons why hot pursuit is so dangerous. First off, it involves pursuit. And second, it's "hot," which means fast.

The key to a safe and productive hot pursuit is control. At all times remain under control. It's just for such a reason as this that we have ourselves a squad car as fine as any in these parts. That vehicle is a finely tuned machine and rises to the occasion every time — just like it did in the manhunt by the lake.

Just as finely tuned are my mind and body. That's the very reason that I keep myself in tiptop condition and avoid high living. The criminal picks the time and place — a lawman's got to be ready. Now, the biggest mistake that's made in hot pursuit is letting your body get ahead of your mind. I have no problem with this because my mind and body work together like a fine machine. But in case you're not so well prepared, just try and remember

"Has Ed Crumpacker worked with you shoulder to shoulder for a lifetime fighting organized crime?"

to think before you act. Think, then act. Think/act. Think/act. Ya' got it? For the seasoned lawman it's second nature. We live it, eat it, sleep it and dream it. Think/act. It could save your life.

Crowd Control

Beating down an uprising is one of the trickiest parts of the business. The reason?

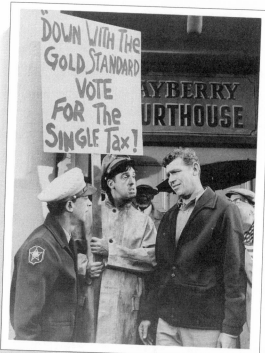

When dealing with wild crowds, the only solution is to nip it in the bud.

Most times it's just good folks who get a little carried away. These folks are the "Demos" in Democracy and they have every right to blow off some steam from time to time.

So what's a lawman to do? The first lesson is to remain respectful. The more calm you can stay as a peace officer the more likely they are to settle down. If you get all worked up on top of their being worked

"You're just full of fun today, aren't you? Why don't we go up to the old people's home and wax the steps?"

up, the whole thing's liable to go *blewy!* and somebody might just get hurt. And that's to be avoided at all costs.

Generally I will appeal to their family values and encourage them to disperse and go on back home. Always talk calmly and sensibly. Try to find their leader and reason with him. Give some ground if you have to, but defuse this situation as best you can. If that doesn't work, bring in the dogs and the gas and haul the whole bunch of 'em off to the "Rock" — that'll cool 'em down.

Working With State and Federal Authorities

From time to time it becomes necessary to work together with law enforcement authorities from other branches of government. We here at the Sheriff's office in Mayberry have a standing policy of doing what we can to uphold the peace at all levels. But we don't take a back seat to any of 'em. In my opinion, if they try to make us take a back seat, we should give 'em the old "deep freeze." For a matter of fact, some of the State Boys could learn a thing or two from the way Andy and I keep the peace in Mayberry.

Now, I'm as big a fan as the next guy of fingerprints and lie detectors and radios. Problem is, once the State Boys and the Feds get these tools they forget the old ways. Many's the time Andy and I've been able to break a case just because we studied on the criminal's M.O. (means of getting organized) and beat him to the punch. I remember a few years back when we busted a big cattle-rustling case with good old common sense. The State Boys just got too caught up in their gadgets to see the forest through the trees. Me and Ange saw it right off. Common sense — that's what did it.

"You're being obtuse . . . I hate it when you're obtuse."

The key to successfully dealing with the Feds and the State Boys is to let 'em think that they're in charge. Just sit back kind'a easy and then *whammo!* — move in for the kill.

No doubt both Andy and I could have moved over to the State level at any time. Thing is, if you start moving the best of the local law enforcement establishment to the State level you're just cutting off your nose to spite your face. Nope. It's better to keep the *cream de la cream* in the trenches and leave the high-falutin' jobs to the desk jockeys in Raleigh.

Here I'm teaching Gomer some of the finer points of "Plain Clothes" detail.

Here the Sheriff and me place our lives on the line without a second thought, in the case of the "Loaded Goat". One false move and Kablooey.

If it ain't broke, don't fix *it* — and law enforcement in Mayberry sure doesn't need to be fixed.

Confidentiality

Few occupations require the level of confidentiality that's needed in law enforcement. One slip and the whole county knows.

Take me, for example. Tell me something and you couldn't drag it out of me with a team of draft horses. Now, sometimes I act like I'm letting the cat out of the bag, but that's just a part of the plan. I knew that the best way to protect that gold shipment *and catch the crooks* was to pass out a little information here and there. (This is called "intelligence" in the law game — though Andy isn't too fond of it. He told me once, "Barn, I don't think you need to use any of that intelligence stuff. You've done all right up to now without any.")

"No longer Barney Fife the man . . . I became Barney Fife the bulkhead."

Summary

I've spent a lot of time here talking about law enforcement and some of the tricks of the trade. Do you know why? Because I'm proud of the way that Andy and I do our job — protecting the citizens of Mayberry. We're just plain, simple men fighting crime with raw courage: strong, determined and fearless. And if you want my best advice, just follow our example.

"Andy, you'll never be lonely as long as I'm around."

"I have a rendezvous with destiny."

4

Self-Defense

No greater love hath man,
than to defend the innocent lamb . . .

I t's the law of the jungle: The strong survive and the weak don't. The only difference between animals and men is that occasionally among Human Beings the predator becomes the protector. That's me — Bernard Fife. Deputy Sheriff. Protector. Animal.

Why the Good Lord placed upon my shoulders the burden of power and strength I don't know. What I do know, though, is that since I was given the gift, I'll bear the responsibility.

Here in Mayberry things are pretty peaceful — usually. Ya' see, Andy is a peace-loving man who believes that everything can be worked out by talking and applying understanding. Take the case of the Wakefield feud. That got straightened out with a little

"A sadder but wiser man — that's me — Barney Fife."

common sense and plain talk. I'll grant you that for the most part that's enough. But it's the velvet hammer that makes it all work. Soft and pretty outside, hard and cold inside. Barney "Velvet Hammer" Fife.

So long as the troublemakers know that the cold, hard steel of Fife is waiting in the wings they'll stay in line. Sorry's the day when that silent threat is gone. Folks don't talk about it. Troublemakers don't ask about it. Criminals don't even think about it. But it's there. Day and night. Rain and shine. Year in, year out. Fife's running the company and crooks need not apply. Ask those two peddlers that I gave the old heave-ho. They'll know better than to try to peddle their vegetables inside the city limits of Barney Fife's town again.

> **"A man confined to prison is a man who has given up his liberty, his pursuit of happiness. No more carefree hours, no more doing whatever you want, whenever you want. No more peanut butter and jelly sandwiches."**

Ol' Roscoe

The discussion of self-defense *a la* Barney Fife starts and ends with ol' Roscoe. Better known to some of the crooks who've seen her in action as the rod, the heater, the blue steel baby, the old persuader, the pistol or the revolver. That baby and me have been down some pretty ugly roads together. But when the dust clears, there we stand, sneering, waiting for the next man fool enough to cross our path.

But the piece of iron a man carries doesn't mean much if he doesn't know how to handle it. These things can get a fella into a lot of trouble, for a matter of fact, if handled improperly. It takes a trained user to avoid the accidental discharge of a lethal firearm. I highly recommend not less than ten minutes per day of fast-draw practice. That's just what I do, and I'm already a highly trained professional in the use of firearms. But to help you out, here are a few tips on using the old heater, if and when the need arises.

"Keep an eye out . . . there's no telling when another beast might come out of the forest."

Prepare Your Weapon

A weapon must be maintained in top condition at all times to be available when duty calls. Failure to do so can result in your weapon failing to fire or, worse, firing when it should not. Over the years I have learned the importance of keeping my weapon clean as a result of several occasions on which it discharged at the wrong time. Now, through my experience, however, this no longer occurs and weapon safety is maintained at all times.

Now, from time to time I'm asked why I carry only one bullet. The reason is quite simple. One bullet, one shot. It sort'a evens up the odds between me and the crooks. But if you decide to go it with only one bullet like me, you must be certain to maintain it in top condition at all times. I'm real proud of my bullet, and as Asa down at the bank says, it's a thing of beauty. I couldn't agree more!

"You're real funny, you are. Why don't you put a red light on your nose and go in the circus?"

Prepare Physically

In addition to the daily practicing of fast-draw technique, a fella should learn to relax the body, but not the mind. Often I'll be hanging around and folks will think I'm taking a nap when all the time I'm physically relaxing while staying mentally sharp. This is a key to being able to use the old persuader to the best advantage.

Staying in shape is also important, though in this regard I have been blessed with a body that turns every ounce of food I eat into raw muscle. If you aren't so fortunate, I recommend a half-hour a day of physical exercise to prepare your body for the responsibility of handling a loaded weapon.

The keeper caged with his prey. Thank you Mr. Izamoto!

Prepare Mentally

The man whose mind is ready to do battle will prevail. Oh, sure, civilians think that the weapon makes the difference. Not true. It's the brain. My brain's the brain of a lawman. At the drop of a hat it's prepared to leap from a dead stop to quick action. Like a steel trap set to spring at the lightest touch of trouble.

To gain this mental preparedness, you should do as I do. I am constantly scanning the scene for signs of trouble. Take a man at face value? You must be kidding. Everyone's a criminal and no one's a criminal. Assume the worst. Think about what you would do if you were attacked — *now!* Prepare your trap and let the criminal fall into it. Think like a predator — stalk . . . wait. Think like Barney Fife.

". . . racing down the highway, just me, the wind and the wheel."

Take Action

After the spring is wound up real tight, let it happen! Snap the body to action. Uncoil the body and lash out! Whirl, spin, cut, turn! Drop the hand to the cold steel of ol' Roscoe and let 'er fly.

That's what's meant when you hear it said that Fife lets his baby do his talking for him. I guess to sum it up you could say that there are three reasons why there's so little crime in Mayberry. There's Andy, and there's me . . . and "baby" makes three.

Mr. Izamoto

To maintain my body in its top condition, I have undertaken the study of judo under Mr. Izamoto of Mount Pilot. Mr. Izamoto always says that to understand judo we must learn that the lion must lie with the lamb. That's like me in Mayberry: Mayberry, the lamb; me, the lion.

A wonderful thing, that judo. Teaches the student to control the awful force that resides in his hands. It sometimes scares me to think of the dreadful power that is welled up within my body. Fortunately, the mental discipline that Mr. Izamoto teaches allows me to live among the citizens — a threat to no one, except the few who would upset the serenity of the oasis we call Mayberry.

"Most of what folks need to learn in life ain't fun to learn."

Summary

Trouble is to be avoided at any cost if humanly possible. Lord knows that if it can be avoided, Barney Fife's gonna try to avoid it. But if it must be dealt with, a man's got to do what a man's got to do. In my experience, being ready, willing and able to create havoc is enough, in most instances, to fend off the problem. But when it isn't, and somebody calls the hand of Barney Fife, rest assured that he's holding the cards to trump 'em. So should you.

"Heaven to Barney Fife'll be a place like a big front porch where I can sit, rock and talk to friends."

A Lawman knows when it's best to call in a highly trained specialist.

"If I let you do 45 today, you'll do 50 tomorrow."

5

Character and a Dignified Life

The highest good of a man
be told, if good character he doth hold . . .

Folks often talk about what makes a person special. You know — what makes him stand out from the crowd. What makes him successful. Well, in my opinion it's got nothing to do with money or social position or good looks. Though I do know some rich folks who are A-OK with me. (Likewise, I know some ugly ones who ain't.) It's more the way a fella handles himself, how he treats others and if you can depend on him. As you can tell, this thing about character is awfully hard to put a handle on. Some folks sum all this stuff about character and dignity up by calling it "class." That's OK. Whatever you call it it's fine so long as you understand that it's what makes good folks good.

"Bernard Fife, M.D. (Mayberry Deputy)."

Since character isn't any one thing, and it's impossible to describe, let me give you a few examples of it. I reckon you'll get the idea of what I'm trying to say.

Character Is Being Yourself

Take Charlie Foley, for example. Charlie runs a clean store and has always had a roof over his head. But rich? Nope. Charlie doesn't always talk right, either. But I never ran into anybody that couldn't understand him. He's nobody's dummy, mind you; he just uses plain words and says what he means. Now, Charlie could throw around big words for this and that cut of beef, or he could use the fancy name for a vegetable. Instead, Charlie calls 'em pot roast and carrots. Charlie doesn't build himself up. He lets his actions do that for him. Let me give ya' an example.

Character Is Forgiving

Once Aunt Bee found she could save a few pennies by buying her meat from one of Charlie's competitors, so she decided to make the switch. Not long thereafter the freezer over at Andy's house broke down and Aunt Bee was gonna lose all of that meat she had just bought. Did Charlie tell Aunt Bee to

"I'm tired of mending Otis's chewed blankets; you'd think he was a cocker spaniel."

Here's Aunt Bee telling Andy how the cow ate the cabbage. He doesn't seem to mind much, though. Does he?

"You see, this is a deadly game; I'm in it for keeps."

take that meat back to where she bought it? Nope. He welcomed Bee back with an open meat locker. He had the upper hand and he knew it. But he was more concerned with helping than getting even. I'll tell you this — she ain't bought so much as a potato from anyone but Charlie since that day. Good things happen to good folks — maybe not right off, but by-and-by.

Character Is Measured by the Heart, Not the Pocketbook

A few years ago right about Christmas time a rich businessman was driving to his home over in Pierce County when he came upon ol' Jubal Fletcher, who'd gotten his car stuck in the ditch by the side of the road. It was a terrible night —

snow and ice — as bad as it gets in these parts. Well, that rich fella in his shiny new car drove right on by Jubal and left him sitting there all cold and stuck. Well, as often happens around here, a local citizen, Jim Lindsey, came by shortly thereafter and pulled Fletch out with his old truck. (Jim went on to become a famous "picker" with Bobby Fleet and his Band With a Beat, by the way. But that's another story.) Together they drove off toward town. A mile or so along the way who do they find but the rich fella with his fancy car stuck up to the hubcaps.

"I'll say it to your face, Otis. You've got a pickled liver."

Without so much as a thought, both Jubal and Jim stopped and pulled the city fella out of the ditch. It's not so much that they pulled him out as it is that they did it happily and without so much as a bad feeling.

Now, you tell me who's more of a success — Jubal and Jim or the fancy city man? Success isn't in wearing clothes from Raleigh booteeks or in college degrees or any of that thing. It comes from what's in your heart.

Character Is Modesty

Now, here's a lesson that's been real hard for me to learn over the years. God was generous with me

→

"Otis is a loveable
Teddy Bear."

→

"I never once
asked Cousin
Andy for any
special consider-
ation when I
applied for the
job of Deputy
Sheriff."

and, from time to time, I've found it hard to keep perspective. Fortunately, Ma and Pa Fife understood their little Barn and helped me find the right balance of confidence and modesty.

I'll never forget when I was a little boy. "Rabbit Fife" is what the kids used to call me. Rabbit — zoom. I could run like the wind as a young 'un. Could'a been because I didn't carry the extra weight of the other kids — I was about fifty-five pounds in sixth grade. Small, but wiry as a cat. In spite of the things I couldn't do because of my size, I could run. I even won a medal for the fifty-yard dash once! I still have it. And I set a lot'a store in that. Matter of fact, too much.

I remember Pa telling me that I shouldn't get all puffed up like a bullfrog because I could run fast, because one day somebody would outrun me. And then where would I be? I didn't pay him much mind, because I knew I could outrun any of 'em.

Then Arnold Winkler moved to town. Big, strong and fast as a polecat. It wasn't long before I learned the meaning of eating crow. But that's all right. What I learned from my Pa still holds and has taught me a life-long lesson: Be modest in victory and proud in defeat. Hearing how good you are sounds a lot sweeter when it's somebody else who's doing the talking.

Character Is Contentment

Reverend Hobart Tucker, Minister of All Soul's Church in Mayberry, said it best when he said that if we all stood in a circle and threw our problems in the middle and then had to take our share of heartaches back, we'd more than likely take back our own. Ya' see, we all have our burdens, but the real test is how we carry those we've been given to bear. Successful folks carry theirs with dignity and joy, and whenever possible, they do what they can to improve their lot. I've never seen a problem yet solved by sulking, have you?

"Losing to a woman . . . jiminy, it's the end of an era."

Character Is Compassion

One time several years ago, Andy and Opie decided that Ope should go out and get a part-time job. Andy thought it'd be good for the boy. Well, as fate would have it, there was a position at Mr. Doakes's Grocery Store as a delivery boy. Opie and Billy Crenshaw both showed up to ask for the job at the same time. Mr. Doakes, being a fair man, told the boys that he'd give 'em a week to prove themselves.

Both boys did a real fine job. Opie and the Crenshaw boy got to talking one day as to how they were going to use the money they earned if they got the job. Opie had his eye on a new bike, and he asked Billy what he would do with the money.

The other boy explained that his family had some hospital bills to be paid. He figured that he could use what he earned to help out. Well, Mr. Doakes told Ope before the end of the week that he was going to give him the job. But Ope, knowing that the other boy was in need, went and got himself fired, leaving the other boy with the job.

Like any pa, Andy was furious that Ope had gotten fired. Only when he heard the whole story did Andy realize that he hadn't raised a good boy — but a fine young man. Enough said.

Character Is Charity

One year I was cleaning up the back room of the Courthouse on the day before Thanksgiving when I hear some talk out in the Sheriff's office. There stands an old man in shabby clothes, obviously down on his luck. I guess folks would call him a bum nowadays. I heard him tell Andy that he'd come up short on bus fare to Atlanta and ended up here in

"When you're an official police escort, you've gotta look smart."

in Mayberry. His family was all in Atlanta waiting for him to share the holiday. Without batting an eye, Andy fished into his pocket and handed over some money to the stranger. The fella pumped Andy's hand and promised repayment, but Andy told him to just pass the favor on some day when he came upon somebody else in need.

"You don't know how to wear the mantle of popularity, do ya'."

Andy Taylor has no big degrees after his name. His bank account ain't big. But his heart is. That's character.

Character Lasts

From what I read in the encyclopedia, folks like Thomas Jefferson and Abe Lincoln had a lot of character. They did things because they were the right things to do, not necessarily because they were the easy thing to do. Same'd be true of Franklin D. Roosevelt and Dwight Eisenhower. Folks are still

Character? If Andy Taylor ain't the most characterful man that ever lived then my name's not Bernard P. Fife.

finding it in their hearts to do what's right, even when it's hard to do. Ya' see, with the invention of all the new machines and the world changing so fast, it's good to know that some things are consistently good. And those things are people. And long after all of the gadgets and modern machines give way to newer and more modern things, people will still be good. That's how folks with character were made, and that's what makes life worth living.

"It wouldn't do for me to stop someone with allspice on my breath."

6

Politics and Public Service

To serve yourself, first serve others . . .

The way I figure it, anybody in daily contact with the biggest public servants around — like Sheriff Andy Taylor, Mayor Pike and Councilman Floyd Lawson — ought to pick up some feel for politics and public service. And if that doesn't qualify me to put in my two cents, the fact that I'm a tax-paying citizen of Mayberry, North Carolina and of the U.S. of A. does.

Politicians confuse me. They need to remember that their job is to serve the public. It sounds simple, but once a man goes to Raleigh it's like he forgets why he was going there. Maybe it's because some of them have been going over there so long that they think they belong there. They forget that

"Keep a good thought."

they were sent there for awhile and that they were supposed to report in occasionally.

The Power of the Incumbent

Take Jim Canfield, for example. I remember my Daddy telling me that he always voted for Mr. Canfield because he was "one of us." He may have started out long ago as one of us, but over the years the good Congressman sure lost touch. He and his entourage would visit Mayberry and he might just as well have been from Montana as Mayberry. Fancy silk suits, big cars, folks hovering about him, testimonial dinners and fund-raisers. We don't do those things in Mayberry. He quit being "one of us" long before he retired. It just doesn't make sense.

Of course, one year we did run Herb Crowley against him. He had a chance, too, right up to when the skeletons in his closet started to rattle. Seems that Jonas Conway told Herb that he'd started giving his pigs tomato juice along with their slop for breakfast, and Herb mentioned this fact to Jess Morgan in passing. At the County Fair, Jess's pig takes first prize, and Jonas's pig takes second. Next thing ya' know Herb is being blamed for giving away the new recipe for slop. Of course, nothing

"The real important stuff belongs to the Smith Brother's Institution in Washington, D.C."

came of Jonas's beef for two reasons. First, there's nothing wrong with two pigs eating the same slop, and two, the judges couldn't find any evidence because Jess's goat ate the tomato juice can.

Congressman Canfield's political machine didn't miss the opportunity to drag Herb Crowley's name through the mud, though. I can still remember the next issue of the *Mayberry Gazette:*

Crowley Implicated in Espionage Scheme:
Probe Thwarted by Destruction of Evidence.
County Officials Promise Full Investigation.

"I got a special place in my heart for 'Old Glory' and what she stands for."

Poor Herb never stood much of a chance after that story hit. Nobody believed that he'd be up to any mischief, but they were so impressed with the Congressman's style that they decided to keep him in office. After that nobody took on the Canfield machine.

Having Mr. Canfield be one of the longest-standing Congressmen wasn't all bad, though. We got all the roads we ever needed and a few we didn't. All our bridges are passable and the National Guard turned out to help us celebrate most anytime we asked 'em. So, all in all, I guess having Mr. Canfield up there didn't really hurt anything.

The Capital Water Supply

I believe that the public water supply in Raleigh causes amnesia. Something happens between the time when we vote for a candidate at the grade school and the time he gets down to business in Raleigh. I have no idea what happens or when it happens. All I know is that something happens during this time.

After the election there's a party where they sip birch beer, munch chips and trade stories about how Farley Thurston's cow only voted three times this year instead of his normal six or seven. Then they pop balloons and throw streamers and carry on like wild for an hour or so. Then they all go home.

Next morning comes and the fella who won the election gives notice at the feed store, or wherever he works, that he's going to Raleigh. He then goes home and packs his bags to go serve his fellow citizens. He says his goodbyes and takes off on the bus to Raleigh. So far, so good.

Fella gets settled in and starts making decisions and voting and *wham* — he has no more idea why he's there than Rafe Hollister's horse. He starts complaining about how small his office is. He holds out for an extra staff member. He hangs around

"There's a little hayseed in all of us . . . some of us cover it up better than others."

with the coat check girl, the information guide and the other folks who work out in the lobby. (He calls 'em "lobbyists.") He rides in the Greensboro Sorghum Festival parade and cuts the ribbon at a new Laundromat in Dobson.

About the only thing that fella forgets to do is the things that he was supposed to do. Yep. I'm convinced it's the water. Just as soon as they quit drinking that clear, clean Mayberry spring water and start drinking the Raleigh chlorinated stuff, their memory draws a blank. It's the water, I tell ya'. It turns 'em all into amnesiacs.

> "A well-maintained bullet shows a lawman's got pride in his status as a keeper of the law."

Voting: A Citizen's Duty

Right, wrong or indifferent, folks need to vote. Us Fifes have always believed that the right to vote is a solemn duty. Never been a Fife who didn't turn out to perform his civic duty to cast a ballot. For a matter of fact, about the only time I remember a Fife not turning out to vote was when Daddy Fife missed in '54 when kidney stones and a weak slate of candidates kept him away. We've always figured that if ya' don't vote, then don't raise a ruckus about what's going on.

Campaign Promises

Over the years I've heard some of the dumbest things said in the name of politics by those that ought to know better. I remember Mr. Lockridge telling folks that if he got elected he would see to it that the town moved into a new era of prosperity and safety. Now, those are some quality lines, except that he was running for the School Board. I've never quite figured out the connection between a good education and my safety. But I guess that's politics. Dumb as it was, it got him elected.

On the other hand, I've heard some of the wisest words from average, ordinary folks whose goal

When it comes to Justice of the Peacing, you won't find a more dedicated public servant than Andy Taylor.

"It's a wise man who knows it's illegal to take the law into his own hands."

was to serve the good folks of Mayberry. I guess that there really is a difference between politicians and public servants. Just for fun, I looked each of these words up in my *Webster's Dictionary.* You might get a kick out of what they say:

pub-lic ser-vice *n* 1: the business of supplying a commodity . . . or service . . . to any or all members of a community 2 : a service rendered in the public interest

pol-i-tics *n* 1 a : the art or science of government b : the art or science concerned with guiding or influencing government policy c : the art or science concerned with winning and holding control over a government

Now, for the definition in *Fife's Dictionary:*

pub-lic ser-vice *n* 1: the dog wags the tail
pol-i-tics *n* 1 a : the tail wags the dog

There it is! Fact of the matter is, it's been right in our faces the whole time. We've been electing politicians instead of public servants. Like

Taking care of young 'uns is a part of public service, too. That Opie's a fine boy, ain't he?

always, I guess it's our fault, not theirs — we keep electing 'em.

The Fife Platform

If Bernard P. Fife ever ran for public office he would keep it simple. None of this stuff about opinion polls and special interests. I'd approach it just like I do the job of Mayberry Deputy. Here's what I'd do:

"Petula Abundalla ain't in the leg, it's in the brain. He gave himself away as a phony right off."

The Bernard P. Fife Platform

1. I'd go in to work at about 8:30 every day.
2. I'd work hard and take a half-hour for lunch.
3. I'd do my best.
4. I'd be honest.
5. I'd be as fair as I could.
6. I'd ask the folks back home for their suggestions.
7. I'd stay for awhile and then come home.
8. I'd try to pitch in wherever I could.
9. I'd promise nothing and try to do some good.
10. I'd follow the Golden Rule.

Now, I know what you're thinking: Anybody could do that. *Exactilioso!* The reason folks elected you in the first place is because they like the way you do things. You shouldn't change *after* you get elected! I guess it's just that Raleigh water supply again that clouds the memory and changes common folks into politicians. They really should do something about that water before it's too late.

In Conclusion, I Must Say . . .

Ever notice how politicians always start to wind up a long-winded speech with that line — "In conclusion . . ."? Seems to me that if the speech was any good to start with they wouldn't have had to tell folks that they were about to finish. People would have been paying attention and would have figured it out on their own.

Anyhow, it seems to me that politics and politicians have been around for a lot'a years and we're likely not to get rid of 'em any time soon. I guess most of the good, common folks of this country will keep right on living their lives and raising their kids and keeping their yards neat in spite of politicians, not because of 'em.

Good folks will go off to work in the morning, work hard, and come home just like they did back in the days of the cavemen. People will do their best and try to improve themselves and then, when they get tired out, they'll turn the world over to their kids. Probably even the politicians can't mess that up. In the end, the common folks'll pick up the slack — they always do.

"You got a uvula. They've got a uvula. I got a uvula. All God's children got a uvula."

"You beat everything, Andy. You know that?"

7

A Gentleman's Wardrobe

*"Clothes make the man" grossly
underestimates the importance of a
good haircut . . .*

I just can't tell you how important it is for you to look your best at all times. The first impression is the one that sticks, so it's real important that you always keep that in mind in picking your clothes.

"Clothes make the man." But that's been said a million times before (a million and one now). For example, not to pick on Ange, but many's the time that I've been ID'd as the Sheriff for the simple reason that I *look* like a Sheriff. What with my spit-shined shoes, genuine 100 percent whiplash cord uniform from Raleigh, crisp shirt and regulation cap, I fit the bill perfectly (not to mention ol' Roscoe, of course).

"I don't look too Ivy League, do I?"

Cleanliness

But looking your best ain't limited to buying fancy clothes. Looking your best means keeping clean and looking fresh and bright. Ma used to always tell us that cleanliness is next to Godliness. If that's so and you grew up in the Fife household, you should rest pretty well assured of a glorious final reward. Because with my Ma, you just couldn't get too clean.

Many's the time when I'd show up for dinner and Ma would march me back up the stairs to wash up all over again. That woman couldn't abide a crusty-looking person at her dinner table. Ernest T. Bass couldn't have gotten within a mile of Ma Fife's table. Not because he was a nut (which he is), but because he carried more top soil than the Mississippi River. Ma could abide a nut, but not a dirty nut.

Another thing that used to stick in my Ma's craw was dirty underwear. I couldn't count the number of times she yelled up the stairs, " . . . and put on clean underwear. In case you get hurt I wouldn't want Doc Bennett to think that we don't keep you young 'uns clean."

"Being allergic to horse hair, when other kids had their picture taken on the back of a pony, I had mine taken on the hood of my uncle's Terraplane."

Take Andy, for instance. You won't find a cleaner man than Andy. And where did he learn it? The Boy Scouts. And, as you can see, that isn't all he learned from Scouting.

"Floyd, do you have to dust me like that? I'm not a diseased crop."

The Boy Scouts

Well, the acorn doesn't fall far from the tree when it comes to me and cleanliness. Back when Andy and me were scouts I learned to quote the Boy Scout Regulations just like I do the North Carolina Criminal Code today. I can still recite the part about cleanliness in the Boy Scout Guide. It said, "Always…ah…be clean…." At least that was the important part. You don't expect a body to remember the whole thing twenty-five years later, do ya'?

That's the difference with us folks with trained memories. We don't clutter our minds with the extra stuff. We just remember the key phrases. Yep. That's what it said all right, "Always be clean." I remember it like it was yesterday! That's a real fine group, those Boy Scouts, and they sure have the right idea about keeping clean.

Speaking of Boy Scouts, Andy and me and Gomer used to take the boys up to the lake for overnight camping trips. Boy, those were great days. Of course, with me being the one with survival training, I was always put in charge of gathering the food and starting the fire (without a match, of course) and getting around without a compass. Other than the times we got lost or nearly died of hunger or frostbite, we had a great time! We need to do that again sometime soon.

Now, back to clothes. To look nice, clothes don't have to be expensive or gaudy. They just have to be kept cleaned and pressed and well cared for. In order to provide a basic starting point to help you, though, I will outline below the basic items that should be the basis of every proper man's wardrobe:

"Yessir Reverend . . . Sin's one thing you can't talk too much about."

Barney Fife's Recommendations
for the Well-Dressed Man

Number One: Two sets of work clothes (In my case this means two complete uniforms, not counting the one that Ernest T. Bass made off with.)

Number Two: One good suit of clothes. Such suit should be versatile enough for both social and professional use. A proper fit for dancing is a must.

Number Three: One white shirt to wear to Sunday church and big dances. The collar should be snug, but not so tight as to shred the skin around your neck.

Number Four: One tie that matches your suit, preferably without hula dancers, clocks, palm trees or stains of any kind. My preference is a bow tie, which we will discuss later.

Number Five: Two pairs of khaki pants to wear on days off and for fishing. No more than one inch of sock should show below the bottom of your pants and the top of your shoes (no more than one-half inch if your socks are yellow).

Number Six: Three button-up shirts for days off. If these are old shirts from item three above, make sure they're not so thin that you can see through them.

"Although I'm a reader of the classics, my taste tends to run to action stories like Moby Dick or Call of the Wild."

Number Seven: Three changes of underwear, including socks. Underwear should still have some elastic and socks should be of a color found in nature. Socks must not sag over your shoe tops.

Number Eight: One pair of work shoes and one pair of Sunday shoes. If you're an undertaker, you only need buy one pair.

Number Nine: One hat for dressing up. Something to match your suit would be nice, but not necessary.

Number Ten: An overcoat for bad weather. Best if you can use it for stakeouts as well. Extra space for food, books, etc., is best. And,

Number Eleven: A jacket for cool weather in the fall and spring. If possible, not the same one you haul fish in from the lake in.

A lot of folks have a lot more clothes than this, but this is all you really need. Everything beyond this is just for show. This basic wardrobe gives you a lot of flexibility. Let's say that you need to attend a function that is neither formal nor casual, like a town band concert (for which I sometimes fill in on my genuine Andre Kostelanetz cymbals). With this wardrobe you just mix and match and always look your best.

"An IQ can be a mixed blessing; some people want it and can't get it. I got it and had to get rid of it."

A Man's Suit of Clothes

I won't go item by item through the list because it kind of speaks for itself. But I will discuss the keystone of every man's wardrobe: his suit of clothes. Now, a suit of clothes is special because it's what you wear to the important occasions of your life, like weddings, funerals and the such. Since these are times when you need to be at your best, it's important to feel good, and to feel good you've got to look good.

The proper suit will be made out of a strong, long-wearing fabric, most likely wool. One way to tell if a suit is a good one before you buy it is to see how heavy it is. If it tips the scale at more than five pounds you've probably got yourself a substantial garment. A suit that's heavy will almost always be long-wearing. Another good test of fine clothes is to rub the material back and forth over your arm hair. If it makes your arm hair stand up with electricity, it's probably made of some man-made stuff and should be avoided.

A suit made of 100 percent wool will wear like iron. The only drawback is that wool can get a bit hot in the North Carolina summer. But for a man to look good, sometimes he has to pay the price. Besides, a suave, confident man always remains cool, even in spite of metallurgical conditions.

The last test of a good suit is how it hangs. Take my salt-and-pepper, for instance. There's a piece of clothing that gilds the lily if ever there was one. Not too tight, not too loose, and, of course, the acid test — the dips. That suit hangs just so in the dips on the dance floor. If Fred Astaire had ol' Barn's salt-and-pepper he wouldn't look quite so

■

"You and Opie ought to go on stage. You're a regular Burt and Squirt."

Barney Fife's Recommendations for the Well-Dressed Man

Haircut a la Floyd Lawson. None Finer in the U.S. of A.

Bow Tie — Safer and better-looking

Fit of the Shirt — Neatly snug, but won't shred your neck

Grade A, 100% Cotton White Dress Shirt — Expensive, but you only live once

Starched Shirt — To keep that fresh look longer

The Old Salt 'n' Pepper. Timeless, Distinguished and hangs just right for doing the Dips on the Dance Floor.

frumpy out there on the floor! Who knows — he might even become a star some day.

Fashion Crazes: In picking out a suit don't be swayed by the styles you see in those magazines over at Floyd's Barber Shop. I've seen many a fella pick out a suit that was all the rage in the big city and in five or ten years it's out of style. Instead, go with old faithful — something like my salt-and-pepper. That suit's thirteen years old and the pants ain't even shiny yet. Fred Goss, the local dry cleaner, says that dollar for dollar, mine's the most durable suit he's seen in years.

A Gentleman's Tie: Now, a tie shouldn't call attention to itself or to its wearer. A tie is something extra that should match your suit, but not make a spectacle of the person wearing it. Hawaiian ties with hula dancers, while they may be OK for a movie star out in Hollywood, don't work near so well for an average citizen of Mayberry. Of course, that's because the average man doesn't have the coordinated ensembles to properly accentuate the contours of horizontal impression. It's all right there in *Today's Man Tomorrow* over at Floyd's.

I prefer bow ties. There are two main reasons why bow ties are more practical than string ties when

"... a **compelsion, you know. Something that you do without knowing that you're doing it—like washing your hands.**"

it comes to your best outfit. Reason one is that they don't get wrinkled and worn-looking nearly as fast as a string tie. String ties are always getting stuck in car doors and small appliances. Not to mention the trouble folks have trying to decide how to get it the right length. Belly button? Belt buckle? First button above your belt? Who knows? Luckily, I've got my uniform tie worn in to where the ridges tell me just where it should fall.

String Ties Are a Health Hazard: One time Gomer was home visiting his cousin Goober for the reunion of Mayberry Union High. Well, Gomer put on his suit and his string tie and he looked presentable, at least for Gomer. So they all go to the dance and stay out 'til near ten o'clock. As they're leaving, Irene Flogg can't get her car started, so Gomer goes over to lend a hand. Him in his good suit and all. Well, he props up the hood and starts to poke the engine, belts and hoses.

"We have two rules here at the 'Rock': #1. Obey all rules. #2. Don't write on the walls as they are hard to clean."

Pretty soon Gomer figures out that one of the belts has come loose and he takes off fixing it. That's just like Gomer, you know — always doing for others. Well, anyway, before long his string tie gets hung up in the fan belt. Quick as a jackrabbit that belt's

Andy's a nice fellow and all; but take a Fife, add a sharp hat, tie and suit and the poor guy just doesn't stand a chance.

➤

"Ernest T. Bass's hostilities are engrained in the deepest recesses of his subconscious id."

going around and around taking Gomer's tie right with it and his head's bobbing up and down like a thirty-pound bass on a twenty-pound line. If Sharon de Spain wasn't there to tell Irene to shut off her car, Gomer would'a sure gotten his head mashed. He came out a bit groggy as it was. He never could get all the grease out'a that tie. There you go — a perfectly good tie wasted because it got caught up in a fan belt. That never would'a happened with a bow tie.

A bow tie shows that the man who wears it is practical. He ain't the type to wear a safety hazard around his neck tempting fate to choke him to death.

Bow Ties — The Cleaner Choice: The second reason wearing a bow tie is better is because you never get gravy on a bow tie. A good tie can last ten years or more unless it's ruined by being covered with gravy, ketchup, ice cream or the such. Ask Fred Goss — I recall him telling us one night over at Andy's while he was courting Aunt Bee that he could give you a pretty good profile of a fella by the stains he took off his tie. So I ask you: Why take all of these chances with string ties? Bow ties are safer, stay cleaner and look every bit as nice as any string tie. That's why I wear one and I've never heard Thel complain. Have you?

"If you flew a quail through this room, every woman would point."

A Gentleman's Hat

Now, there's not much I'm gonna say about hats except to point out a bad habit many folks have — they put other people's hats on their heads. Don't put my hat on your head. I don't like someone else wearing my hats. My Ma was the same way. If you're in this bad habit I have one piece of advice for you — nip it in the bud! Now!

The Uniform Dress Code

Now, if you ever need to wear a string tie, like I do with my uniform (Section 23, Paragraph 2 of the Uniform Dress Code for County and Municipal Employees, 1963 Revision) the first lesson you will learn real quick is to always use a tie bar. The regulations speak directly to this point:

Section 23, Paragraph 2, Subsection 3(a)(1) reads as follows:

▬

"Every thinking pioneer and inventor has suffered the same kind of ridicule."

3(a)(1) Approved Uniform Accessories — Neckwear. All employees of all counties and municipalities within the State of North Carolina shall wear such accessories, and only such accessories, to neckwear as are approved in this subsection. All accessories to neckwear shall be not less than one and one-half inches in length and not more than four inches in length. They shall be no wider at the widest part than one-half inch, nor shall they be any less wide than one-eighth of an inch. They shall be made of a metallic material including, but not limited to, steel, stainless steel, gold, brass, copper, or platinum. No accessories to neckwear will be approved within this subsection if made of plastic, cloth or any animal derivatives such as bone or ivory.

At no time shall any neckwear described in Section 23, Paragraph 2 be worn without the use of an approved neckwear accessory as permitted by this section.

Penalties for violation of this subsection shall be according to the uniform guidelines for violation of this Code as stated in Section 14 hereof.

As you can plainly see, it's necessary to employ a tie bar at all times when wearing a string tie. Ask Gomer. He'll tell you it makes good sense.

A Gentleman's Footwear

The final part of a gentleman's outfit should be a good pair of shoes. Of course, a man should have a special pair of shoes for work and a separate pair to go with his suit.

Work shoes fall into two categories — safe or comfortable. The best pair of work shoes have a steel toe and crepe soles. But these extra special features cost a pretty penny. Take the shoes I wear with my uniform, for example. They're the finest money can buy.

A short time ago, a shoe salesman was passing through town, so he got himself a room for the

"A fella who doesn't honor the USA in a proper way, and who doesn't get a little misty when he hears Patriotic songs, ain't no friend to Barney Fife."

"If you don't sell it to me (ice cream soda), I'll just get it somewhere else."

night over at the Mayberry Hotel. Well, one thing led to another and the folks got to gossiping that the fella was really a talent scout instead of a shoe salesman. Before long, the word's all over town that a talent scout is at the hotel looking for acts.

Pretty soon there are all kinds of people outside the shoe salesman's room. As you might expect, things got a bit rowdy out there in the hall, what with the folks being all excited to get their chance to audition.

After restoring order, I settled in to talk to Wilbur Finch, eastern regional sales manager for the Manhattan Shoe Company. (I thought he might enjoy a harmonica tune while we talked.) As it turns out he had with him right there in the hotel a pair of size 7½B black leather work shoes with steel toes, steel shanks, crepe soles, steel heel taps and steel-tipped shoestrings. I had never seen a finer pair of shoes in my life. I knew right then and there that I had to have them. To top it all off, they fit me perfectly the very first time I put them on my feet. The only problem was that they cost $5.50. For Barney Fife to spend $5.50 on a pair of shoes is unimaginable. Yeah, that's what I thought, too. But, as Mr. Finch says about shoes, "They're the body's chauffeurs. For $5.50 don't you deserve a Cadillac?"

I thought about those shoes for a while and then marched over to my room and got my mad money right out of my Bible (between Ezekiel and Daniel). It was a big step, but sometimes a man's just got to step out and take a chance. Buying those shoes was one of the best decisions I ever made.

A man in my position has to look good while all the time being ready to take physical action if the need arises. My steel-reinforced black leather work shoes fit the bill perfectly. And Mr. Finch even threw in a jar of Melotonin shoe paste to boot. It was just a deal too big to resist. It was just my crazy side coming out, I guess.

A Gentleman's Socks

A good pair of socks can make a big difference in how a fella feels. Now, some socks are so bulky that it makes it nearly impossible for you to get a good fit with your shoes. When you put your foot in, things bunch up until there's a big wad of sock up above the top of your shoe strings. And hurt! For crying out loud, there's nothing that can hurt a man like a pair of bunched-up socks.

"If I weren't one to let bygones be bygones, I'd bring up how Andy snuck in to escort the reigning Miss Apricot a few years ago . . . after I spent $3.50 for a new pair of shoes."

Wool socks are probably the worst offender when it comes to bunching up at the top. To make matters worse, wool socks simply can't be made to be cool, which, of course, is what you're looking for in the winter. But in the heat of the summer the smell of a pair of sweaty wool socks can stop a draft horse in its tracks. When you think about wool socks it sure makes you appreciate cotton. But that brings up a totally other problem.

Cotton socks can be so thin that they hardly do your feet any good at all. You can feel every crack and cranny in a pair of too-thin socks. You'd be better off wearing none and saving the trouble of doing the extra wash.

Another type of socks to avoid are those shiny, slippery kind. They sag around your ankles, and your feet keep slipping out of your shoes. You know — the kind Gomer wore the night he and Mary Grace triple-dated with us. I've never beheld a worse sight than those yellow socks with Gomer's leg hairs sticking through. Ugly's what they were. But that ain't even the worst part. He also had on new shoes. Between the new shoes and slick socks, it was like he was on roller skates the whole night. And ugly!

"I thought about buying a ring 'the Star of Peoria' from Newton Monroe for Thelma Lou."

In a word, socks can't really do much *for ya'* but keep your feet comfortable. They can, however, make ya' look pretty stupid. I know it seems like a little thing, but it's the little things that make the difference between a Gomer Pyle and a Cary Grant. Between a Dud Wash and a Frank Sinatra. Between a nobody and a Barney Fife.

As I said before, there are a thousand things I could comment on about the right way to dress and groom yourself, but the final one I will discuss is the value of a good haircut.

"I'm thinking of replacing the fake fur that I bought from Newton Monroe with a pineapple slicer."

A Good Haircut

There's an old saying around these parts that a man can only look as good as his haircut. There's a lot of truth to that. Now, we folks in Mayberry have been fortunate to have Floyd Lawson cutting our hair here for nearly thirty years. He's cut three generations of many a family's hair.

There's one thing you can rest assured of and that's that a visit to the barber shop will improve not only your looks, but also your

Here I am in casual attire. Note the primo *haircut and stylish plaid shirt I've selected.*

That Ellie Walker's a fine example of Mayberry pulchritude.

disposition. Somehow you just feel like a new man with a trimmed head of hair. In any event, if clothes make the man, a good haircut makes the clothes. And nobody makes a haircut like Floyd Lawson.

Women

As you can see, I haven't addressed women's clothes and the such, mostly because that ain't the sort of thing I'm qualified to be writing about. But if you're a woman and you're reading what I've said about men, you can apply just about everything I've said to women. If that ain't enough, look at the fine women of Mayberry like Thelma Lou and Ellie Walker and Miss Crump. Wear what they wear and keep yourself up like they do and you won't miss the mark by much.

"You belong in the funny papers, you know that? Give you a wig and a dress and you're another Emmie Smaltz."

In closing, let me say that it's not the shell that makes a peanut good. Nor is it the clothes that make a person good or bad. But since you've got to wear clothes anyway and since soap's only a nickel a bar, why not look your best? It just makes good sense to me.

"Andy Taylor don't run things so much by the book as by the heart."

"Once all the pieces fall together, you'll see the whole picture."

8

Food and Nutrition

Show me a man with a hearty appetite, and I'll
show you a happy man . . .

Us Fifes have always been big eaters. Of course, we never have any problem with fat, because everything we eat goes right to muscle. We're little, but lean. My Mother's the same way. All goes to muscle. You know what I mean? Well, because we like to eat we're all quite the experts on eating and what's good and what ain't.

I thought that I'd spend a few minutes here and talk about the Mayberry cuisine and some of my favorite dishes. If you're not hungry when you start reading I'm sure you will be when you're done. Matter of fact, I think I'll whip up a little snack before we even get started. I really haven't had a bite since I had the "Big Boy" breakfast this morn-

"Off duty? When is a lawman really off duty?"

100

ing at the diner (all you can eat for $.95), and it's a quarter to eleven now.

OK, I'm back. I just put together a little something to tide me over: a couple'a cold chicken legs with some extra barbecue sauce on the side, a slice of mozzarella pizza, a cut of rhubarb pie and a glass of milk. Andy said Aunt Bee was going to be late with lunch today (12:15), so this should tide me over. Now, where were we? Oh, yeah. We were talking about food and nutrition and the such.

The Importance of a Regularly Scheduled Mealtime

To a person like me, eating is real important. You see, being on the slender side, I have to be awful careful to not upset the metabolistic balance of my body. Us Fifes run like clocks — never slow down. My Ma had a high metabolism; I'm the same way. Many of you folks are no doubt the same. Now, some folks find it best to eat one or two bigger meals and one small meal during the day. That's where the difference comes in. For me to avoid afternoon sinking spells (which is a must in the law enforcement game — do you realize that according to *The Police Gazette* more than 37 percent

"We're going to turn Mayberry into the gateway to Monte Carlo."

of all crime is committed between lunch and dinner?), I need to eat several smaller, well-spaced meals each and every day. Just to show ya' what I mean, let me go through a typical day in the life of the Fife digestive system.

The Barney Fife Six-Meal-a-Day Plan

Morning: Normally, I start with a light breakfast. My favorite is: orange juice, a bowl of cereal, a stack of wheats, three eggs over (not runny), bacon on the crisp side, white toast buttered, hash brown potatoes and coffee. This'll usually get me through the better part of the morning, but after I make my morning rounds I always try to pick up a midmorning snack — something like a danish or doughnut. If I don't fill in with a danish or something, my hunger'll be raging by the time lunch comes around. Pity the criminal that runs across a Fife who's missed his midmorning snack. It just makes me plain ornery.

The Lunch Schedule: I like to eat lunch pretty much right on schedule every day. You see, us Fifes have a finely tuned system and a half an hour either way can throw me all off and give me a *grande* headache.

> "**I** before **E**, except after **C**; **E** before **N** in chicken . . . I always forget that one."

From time to time Andy will tell me I'm being difficult for wanting to eat on a regular schedule. Shows what appreciation he's gained over the years for the Fife digestive system.

The Bluebird (. . . and Juanita): My favorite time to eat is at 11:45. If you eat at 11:45 you can beat the rush and get a booth at the Bluebird. This allows you to avoid having to sit too close to the kitchen, where the heat coming off of the French frier can make ya' raise a sweat. It doesn't seem to bother Goober, though. I guess compared to the business end of a Chevy, a French frier ain't bad. Nevertheless, hardly a good way to eat your lunch — sweating and all. In any event, for under a dollar (a tip for Olive included) a man can refuel the old boiler. Tell you the truth, I've never figured out how Olive does it. But she does it day in and day out. That's what you call a true professional. Good ol' Olive — bless her heart.

"If this is practicing for marriage, I'm going to study up to be a hermit."

Lunch With Aunt Bee: Now, I stick to 11:45 whether I'm going to the diner (and my sweet Juanita) or if I'm eating somewhere else. A good deal of the time Aunt Bee brings us lunch down to the Courthouse.

There's just not a better sight than to look out the window and see Aunt Bee coming down the street with that picnic basket on her arm. No telling what's going to be in that basket from one day to the next — sweet potato pie, chicken salad sandwiches, chocolate cake, bean salad and a thousand other things a hungry man would give his eyeteeth for. So long as she's not packing any of those pickles of hers, Aunt Bee can feed me anything. But she needs to leave the pickle-making to Clara Edwards — Aunt Bee's taste of kerosene.

Brown-Bagging It: On those rare days when I don't eat at the Courthouse or at the diner, I fix myself a little something. Usually two sandwiches and a Mr. Cookie Bar will do the trick. Whenever I get the chance I'll put my sandwiches on salt-rising bread and have myself a real treat. For a little afternoon pick-me-up I'll throw in an extra sandwich and an extra helping of dessert, because a slender, high-spirited person like me needs a sugar pick-me-up in the middle of the day. Keeping the peace is a tough enough job on a full stomach — it's near impossible on an empty one.

Of all the gall. Feeding my lunch to that dog threw off my Digestive System for three days.

Dinner. Now, generally after two fairly light meals for breakfast and lunch, I help myself to a more-substantial dinner. Wherever it is that I eat, I make sure that I get filled up at dinner. About the only time I'll hold back is if Thel and I go out for dinner. Even though we go Dutch, the bill for a full-course dinner out can be highway robbery. Why, sometimes they'll add twenty cents to the price of a meal just because you're ordering it after 5:00. (But I must say that it's incredible what you can get over at Morrelli's for $1.85: minestrone soup that's absolutely delicious and the Pounded Steak *a la*

"How can you move to South America? You know Opie and Aunt Bee don't speak a word of South American."

Morrelli, which is really pounded right before your eyes in their open kitchen. Of course, the shrimp cocktail is extra. But who could eat it anyway? The minestrone and the pounded steak are enough to fill a horse.)

I've often thought that there must be a regulation in the North Carolina Code for eating establishments that would put the kibosh to price-raising after 5:00. I haven't found anything yet, but I'm still looking. The very idea of setting your prices by the clock! If there ain't a law, there should be. Well, you can bet I'll have the old nose in the books again tomorrow looking at those regulations. The very idea!

"I blew my chance for the big ball of wax in high school . . . I had a connection with the FBI. My father had a friend who did a lot of plumbing in Washington."

A Little Something to Sleep On: I like to take a snack late at night, around 9:30 or so. Me being a night owl (Sometimes my head doesn't even hit the pillow 'til quarter before eleven.), I need something to put me over the top for the night. Most folks don't realize how many calories they burn in their sleep. Especially us folks with high metabolistic rates. Tapioca pudding and hot chocolate is my favorite. They top me off and I sleep like a baby. Of course, all of us Fifes are sound sleepers. When I was a young 'un, Pa once slept right through the whole night with Cy Hudgins's pig stuck under our front porch. Made the awfulest racket — enough to wake the dead, but not Daddy Fife. Clear conscience and hot chocolate — they'll do it every time.

Sunday Dinner at Andy's

Few traditions known to modern man exceed the simple joy of eating pot roast with Aunt Bee, Andy and Opie on a Sunday afternoon. It's not just the pot roast (though Aunt Bee's pot roast is known all the way over in Pierce County). It's the people. Breaking bread with friends is one of the great remaining joys of life. Every week we finish off by having coffee and dessert out on the front porch while we rock, relax and talk. Sometimes for a special treat we'll make up a tub of strawberry ice cream and take turns turning the crank. Even Mr. Tucker, the big city fella, enjoyed this. I often think that if Eisenhower and Stalin and all those folks would've eaten some of Aunt Bee's pot roast and had dessert out on the front porch, the world would be a safer place. It's just a thought.

"We should be prepared to search for Neal in case he comes viz-a-viz. You know, hand to hand."

Picnic Lunches at Myers' Lake

Mayberry weather is just perfect for picnics about nine months out of the year, and, due to quick action by the North Carolina Department of Agriculture, the mosquito population has been at a low for a good many years now. These are two of the main ingredients for a perfect picnic. To these, you add cole slaw, cold turkey sandwiches, a relish tray of fresh cut carrots and celery, pecan pie and iced tea and you're well on your way to a memorable afternoon communing with nature. Finally, you add a friend like Andy and two beautiful women — Thel and Helen — and you've got yourself as fine a day as you would want. More folks should try it more often. It's sort of a lost art.

"Oh, you're funny, you are. Why don't you put a flower in your lapel and squirt water."

Cooking at Mrs. Mendelbright's Boarding House

As you all well know, cooking on the premises of Mrs. Mendelbright's is strictly prohibited. However, I'm sure that that rule was established to keep traveling salesmen and the like from cooking out over an open fire in the guest rooms. That rule wasn't ever meant to apply to a long-term boarder like me. I just keep my burner out of sight from

Mrs. Mendelbright so as not to make an issue of it. But with me not being a short-termer, well, I reckon she really wouldn't apply the rule to me even if she found out. That once when she got sore at me it only happened because the chili Andy and me was cooking started to smoke. To this day, I'm really not sure why it did that. Guess it must've been the recipe for "Red Hot Real Mexicano Chili" from the High School Spanish Club that I used — *ole!*

I've heard of getting in trouble because of a smoking gun . . . but a smoking pot of chili?!

Cooking for One

The key to cooking for one over a single-eye burner is planning. With just the one burner there ain't a lot of flip-flopping you can do. It's pretty much warm something up and eat it. The trick is what my Ma used to call "doctoring" up foods that otherwise might be a bit bland — like baked beans, beef stew and weiners. With a little imagination you can come up with some fine dishes that you can easily make for one, and what's more, they're cheap and easy. (Not that I spare the expense when it comes to the old digestive system — to keep a fine piece of equipment like me running in tip-top form ya' can't be running on the cheap. Barney Fife takes High Test all the way.)

To get you started in the right direction on eating right, I've even included a few of my favorite recipes for one. Each of them can be made on a one-eye burner using only one pan. I know they work because I came up with 'em myself. *Bon appetit.* (That means "good eating" in Spanish.)

Cream of Tomato With Oyster Pillows

Ingredients:
1 can (10 3/4 ounces) of Cream of Tomato Soup
1 can of Milk (non-fat)
Twenty to Thirty Oyster Crackers

Prepare:
First open the can. Heat up your burner and make
sure that it aint too hot. If it is,you'll scorch
your soup and get all kinds of chunks of tomatoey
stuff in your soup. Pour the contents into the pan.
Slowly add one can of milk by mixing it in a bit
at a time while stirring constantly. Allow the soup
to get real near a boil (Be careful to not let it
boil, or it'll suds up and spill over your pot.
Let it cook just short of a boil for five minutes
and take it off the burner. Pour a bowlful into a

For a light, yet filling meal, you can't beat this Fife favorite.

big bowl. Drop half of the crackers (approximately 15)
into the bowl of soup. Save the rest to eat withyour
soup. A robust meal for the working man. Serves one,

Serving suggestions:
Extra good with a pastrami-on-rye or peanut butter-and
jelly sandwich.

Cream of Tomato With Oyster Pillows

Pasta and Cheese With Weiner Slices

Ingredients:
One package (7 3/4 ounces of Macaroni and Cheese)
One cup of Water
Three tablespoons of Margarine
One-Third cup of Milk (non-fat)
Four Weiners

Prepare:
Heat up your burner 'til it's pretty hot. Add the
cup of water and get it to boiling. Open the noodles
part of the package of macaroni and cheese and pour
them into the boiling water. Cook 'em until they're
nice and soft(but not mushy). Drain the extra water
off by making a little crack between the lid and
the pot. Add the cheese sauce to the drained
macaroni and stir. Then add the milk and the margarine
and stir some more. Take the weiners and slice them
up about the size of checkers. Put the weiner slices
in the pan with the macaroni and cheese mixture. Cook
at about half heat for five minutes. Serves one.

This one's really healthy: It has three of the main food groups covered!

Serving suggestions: Instead of weiner slices, throw in
some fully cooked country ham. De-licious.

Pasta and Cheese With Weiner Slices

For those cold nights when you need a hearty man-sized meal, take it from me: This one's Mucho Good.

```
Chicken a la Fife

Ingredients:
One can (10 3/4 ounces) of store brand Chicken a la King
One can (6 ½ ounces of store brand Peas

Prepare:
Heat your burner slowly until it's not quite hot. Then you
open the can of chicken a la king and pour it into the
pot. Let this simmer (just sit there cooking without
boiling) for about five minutes, give or take. Open the
can of peas and pour them a little at a time into the
chicken a la king you're heating up. Let the two main
ingredients cook for another five minutes and then serve
by pouring over a slice of salt-rising bread. Serves
one.
Serving suggestions: Trade out the salt-rising for a
buttermilkd biscuit for a new taste sensation.
```

Chicken a la *Fife*

I don't keep a card for the next one. I can cook this up by heart, but here are the directions, written out:

~~~~~~~~~~~~

Aunt Bee's Leftover Chicken and Dumplin's

Ingredients:

One jar of Aunt Bee's Leftover Chicken
    and Dumplin's
You don't need anything else.

Prepare:

. . . by warming your burner up, but don't get it real hot. Pour in that jar of leftovers and just let it warm

"You're almost as funny as Floyd. You know that? Why don't you two team up? Call yourselves Frick and Frack."

a bit at a time. To make up for the steam, put in a little bit of water if you want to.

When it's all warmed through, pour it on your plate and go to eating. Mighty fine meal. If you don't know an Aunt Bee or somebody who can cook like her, find one and fast. My suggestion is that you consider mothers-in-law, grandmas, aunts or just other good women who can cook up a storm. You're missing some fine vittles otherwise.

Serves one.

Serving Suggestions:
Don't change a thing. You can't improve on Aunt Bee!

~~~~~~~~~~~~

"I replaced the pea in the whistle, but I ain't gonna charge you for it."

9

Personal Finances

Money, while not a necessity,
certainly is a convenience . . .

Anytime I get to talking about money I have to recall the rules for money that Daddy Fife taught me many a year ago. They were simple and to the point:

Rule 1. *Never spend more than you have in cash.*

Rule 2. *Never borrow (except for a house).*

Rule 3. *Never lend.*

Rule 4. *Make a budget and stick to it.*

Rule 5. *Always give away the first fruits.*

In the Fife household these rules had the same weight as the Ten Commandments and the Golden Rule. They weren't to be broken. And for good reason. If you follow these rules, money, though maybe

"I don't know how I can face the future knowing that there's eight quarts of pickles in it."

not plentiful, will be used as wisely as possible. And that's about the best you can do in this particular area.

Rule 1
Never Spend More Than You
Have in Cash

Take Rule 1, for instance. It seems to be obvious, but folks just don't pay it heed. Daddy Fife believed that the worst thing that ever happened to the world economy was the creation of credit.

Giving credit started in Mayberry years ago when Charlie Foley, the grocer, started allowing folks to carry a balance on account. Now, he's been doing that ever since I was a boy. The reason he started giving credit was so that the farmers who lived outside of town could send in their hired help or their kids or whoever to pick up supplies. Of course, no farmer is going to send real money with his hired help, so he worked out a deal that he would come in every week or two to settle up.

There was never any intention of allowing folks to spend money they didn't have. But pretty soon, *everybody* was carrying a balance Now, this didn't make any sense at all, but it was convenient. They

"A choir without its tenor is like a star without its glimmer."

would've been better off inconvenienced than in debt. Right? Daddy Fife wasn't any fool, ya' know.

Mother Fife's New Easter Dress: One time when I was young I went to the market with my Ma. She had spent every spare minute for weeks making herself a new dress to wear for Easter. She had worn her other one for the last six years and was all excited about having something new. Well, two days before Easter we went to Weaver's Department Store. The only thing left to finish on that dress were the buttons and the bow in the back.

So we're shopping and she finds just the right buttons and bows. The only trouble is, they're fine goods from Raleigh and they were real expensive. The total came to $2.97, but she only had $2.00 with her. Well, Mr. Weaver tells her that she can come by and make up the difference when she has it. Do you think she'd have any part of that? No siree.

Ma told me that there wasn't a do-dad made that she would borrow money for. And besides, there were many more-important things to be done with a dollar than to buy imported buttons and lace for a Sunday dress.

"I'll just melt into the shadows. He won't know I'm within a hundred miles."

Ma wore the old dress again that Sunday. She finished the new one and wore it the next year (and the six after that). I'll never forget that dress and how pretty Ma looked in it. Nor will I forget the lesson she taught me while she was making it.

Rule 2

Never Borrow

Rule 2 is really just an extra piece of Rule I. Seems as though folks just get caught up in having things. But there really ain't many things you need bad enough to buy them with money you don't have. At least that's how us Fifes were taught.

We were taught that borrowing money was the root of many a problem. Ya' see, if you borrow money to buy something, sooner or later that thing will wear out or need fixing. But even after it's used and broken and all the newness has rubbed off, you still owe the money you borrowed.

Just for fun, say you want a new fishing reel. Well, all of the time you're saving up, you're dreaming of how nice it'll be to have that new reel. You tell your friends about it and you stop by Weaver's to look at it and you can almost feel it in your hands. It's exciting. You're not thinking about the work,

"Nimbleness, agility and dexterity is the key to hand magic."

you're thinking about that new reel. Then the big day comes and you've saved enough to buy that new reel. You're so proud. You march into Ben's store and lay your money down and get that reel you've been working and saving and scrimping for. But when you get it it's yours. Nobody else's. And when you fish with it the only thing you have to think about is how wonderful it is, not how you're gonna pay the next payment on it.

Concentration is no less important in fishing than it is in Deputying. By the way, ain't that a beautiful fishing rod? And it's all paid for!

Nobody else knows just how wonderful that reel is. Everybody else just sees a fishing reel. You see your hard work, your self-discipline, your dreams — as well as your shiny new reel. Now, if you were to have walked off with that reel on credit, things would have been quite different. Since you didn't save and pay cash, you now have to pay for it after you have it. Every time you look at that new reel all you see is the bill you get every month until it's paid for. It's sort'a like having somebody bite the end off your raspberry snow cone and suck all the juice out. It takes all the fun out of it!

The Buying a House Exception: Now, there's one exception to the no-borrowing rule — it's OK to borrow money to buy a house. Buying a house when the time is right is important to setting up a proper household, and a proper household is good for a family. A family needs a house. Young 'uns need a backyard to play in, and ma's and pa's need hedges to trim, windows to wash and walls to paint. Teenagers need grass to mow and chores to do. Working together to make a house a

"The widow Saunders has been stepping out with a dish towel salesman from Raleigh who drives a wire-wheeled coupe."

Friends and family can turn any building into a wonderful home!

121

home brings a family together, and anything that brings a family together is A-OK with us Fifes.

Rule 3
Never Lend Money

If you believe Rule 2, the reason for Rule 3 should be pretty clear. It's been my experience that no good ever came of lending folks money. If you lend money, only one of two things can happen, and they're both bad.

"I did my part to defeat the dreaded Hun. This corporal and me was responsible for over 3,000 books in the PX Library on Staten Island. But I'd rather not talk about it."

First off, let's assume that you lend money and you don't get paid back. Well, in that case you're going to be miserable for having made the loan and mad because you got stiffed. In both cases, you're not going to be too pleased with the fella. Assuming that you loaned the money to somebody you liked to start with, the chances that you're going to lose that friendship are real good. Now tell me — how much money is a friendship worth?

Mayor Pike — Real Estate Lender: A few years back Mayor Pike had a brother-in-law who was making big money in real estate over in Mount Pilot. He had bought himself a big new car, fancy clothes and all of the trimmings. He was living the high life.

So Mr. Big Real Estate Man asks Mayor Pike to lend him two hundred dollars. Now, two hundred dollars is a lot of money, even to Mayor Pike. But what was he to do? He felt that he had no choice but to help his brother-in-law out.

As you might suspect, things in the Mount Pilot real estate market hit the skids. Mr. Big Shot starts to come up short and tells the Mayor that he's not going to be able to pay him back. So now the good Mayor's in a fix. His savings are lost and he has to choose whether to deal with his brother-in-law as kin or as a rounder. That's a pretty tough choice since no matter what he decides the fella's still going to be sitting across from him at Christmas dinner, and he's still going to owe him two hundred dollars. He might forgive the debt, but he'll never forget. And the Mayor's a pretty forgiving fella down deep. But it'll just never be quite the same between them.

Loaned Money Is Never Really Repaid: Lending money is a bad idea even if you get repaid! When you lend money to another person, the basis of your relationship shifts from your heart to your wallet. And I don't know if you've noticed it, but folks are funny

"Let old Barney take you to the land of Rhythm."

123

when it comes to their wallets. Anyhow, even if you get paid back, most folks will believe that they're owed something more. And you never will get 'em repaid in full.

Whatever happens in money lending, it's bad. Like Bill Shakespeare said:

"The tears on my pillow bespeak the pain that's in my heart."

> *Neither a borrower nor a lender be;*
> *For loan oft loses both itself and friend . . .*

I guess what was true in England fifty years ago is still true in Mayberry today. Lending money just doesn't work out. (I guess you never expected to hear Barney Fife quoting Shakespeare, did ya'? Why not? What do ya' think I am — some jerk?)

If you're just bound and determined to take on somebody else's money problems, just make it simple: *Give 'em the money and don't expect it back.* If they do ever give it back it'll be a surprise, and as Ma Fife said, "It's better to be surprised than disappointed."

Rule 4
Make a Budget and Stick to It

Now, I'm a big fan of ol' Rule 4. The Fife family has always been frugal. Waste not, want not, and the best way to see to it that you don't come up short is to do careful budgeting. You just gotta plan.

Nobody would set out to raise pigs and feed 'em all of the corn in the first month. Nobody would paint a fence and put three coats on the first section and leave no paint for the rest. It's no different in dealing with your money affairs.

I, for one, make a monthly budget in January of every year and stick to it for the whole year — come rain or come shine. Just to give you an idea of how to go about this, let me show you my budget as an example of how to do this right.

~~~~~~~~~~~~

"I always enjoy walking over to the Grand and watching them change the marquee."

<pre>
                    Bernard P. Fife's
                    Monthly Budget
                    _____

WHAT COMES IN:
    City of Mayberry (Deputy Pay)............$475.00
    Mayberry Bank (Savings Account Interest)... 8.56
    Mayberry Bank (Christmas Club Interest),.... .80
                                              -
                                    Total $484.36

WHAT GOES OUT:
    Reverend Hobart Tucker (See Rule 5).......$47.50
    Mrs. Mendelbright (Room Rent)............ 24.00
    *Food....................,................135.00
    Taxes....................................115.00
    Insurance.................................28.00
    Electricity, Gas &Water (Included in Room Rent)
                          ....0.00
    New Uniforms and Clothes...... . .. .30.00
    Vacation (Raleigh, YMCA Deluxe Room w/Window12.00
    Fishing License..........................1.00
    Eleono.a Poultice (Voice lessons)............6.00
    Mr. Izamoto (Judo)..........................6.00
    Subscription (True Blue Detective).......... 1.00
    Dues (Lodge, etc.)........................... 2.00
    Dates and Entertainment ($5.00 per week)....10.00
    **Savings ($6.00 per week)..................24.00
    **Christmas Club ($2.50 per week)..........10.00
    Gifts, etc.................................10.00
    ***Money for a Rainy Day 22.86
                                              -
                                    Total $ 484.36
</pre>

The Bernard P. Fife Monthly Budget

* Figuring one meal per week at Thelma Lou's and one meal per week (Sunday dinner) with Andy, Aunt Bee and Opie.

** Even though I have owned a share or two of stock in my day, I found that deputying and stock analyzing don't allow ample time to do either one properly. I remember telling Andy once that if you're not a "plunger," then the stock market's not the place for you. You know what'll happen? You'll get killed! Exactilioso. Killed. Barney Fife's made his decision, and that's why my holdings are over in Cyrus Tankersley's safe at the Mayberry Bank. They don't call 'em safes for nothing, ya' know.

*** This is the place I got the money to do my big deal with the Mayberry Record Company. Andy passed, but me and Floyd and some of the others did OK.

~~~~~~~~~~~~~

A word to the wise: When bill-paying time rolls around, put your savings account right in line behind the Lord. After all, next to the Big Fella Upstairs, who deserves to be taken care of more? I look forward to being able to afford a comfortable retirement when my crimefighting days are over. Nobody else's going to do it for ya' and there won't be many folks chipping in for ya' if you're old and broke. Now's the time to deal with that — while the money truck is still making regular deliveries.

Now, let me make it clear that this is just an illustration of the type of budget you might want

"It's guys like you who laughed at Edison, the Wright brothers, and Buzz Fluhart*."

* Buzz Fluhart discovered hexes.

to make. Of course, your numbers and categories might be different, but it's the same idea. Say, for example, that you made two hundred dollars more a year than I did. Well, you could just change your budget to fit. So the idea stays the same even if the numbers change. Ya' got it?

Over Budget?: Now, as the year progresses, it's important to look at your budget every month or so. If you're getting off track — say inflammation causes Olive to raise prices at the diner or Mrs.

Mendelbright raises your rent (or even lowers it, which she says she's considering) — then you can make adjustments. But if you get over budget, nip it! *Nip it in the bud!* Right now! But don't forget Rule I. If you come up short, cut your spending. Skip that movie next week or go to the diner instead of Morrelli's. Whatever you do, stay within your budget. If you don't, you'll find yourself in terrible shape at the end of

Sometimes when I take my deposits to the Bank, Gomer walks along with me . . . just to be extra secure.

the year and wanting in the worst way to violate Rule I. Nip it! Nip it! Nip it! If you do get off budget, you'll know in time to do something about it. That happened to me a few years ago, but luckily, I was able to pick up a few extra bucks selling real estate for a time. That got me back to being a solvent. From that day on I learned the importance of keeping up with my budget and making adjustments as necessary to avoid having to moonlight to make ends meet.

At the end of the year, look at how ya' did. Before you make your budget for the next year, see what went according to Hoyle and what got off track. Now, by doing this you'll be able to adjust next year's budget as necessary. From then on it's *no problemo, amigo.*

Rule 5
Always Give Away the First Fruits

Rule 5 speaks for itself, doesn't it? Now, I don't really think that it matters how you choose to do your giving or to whom. Church is nice, but there is a whole world of other worthy causes. In the Fife family there was nothing that could come before returning to the Lord. And many was the day when there wasn't much to give. But somehow that never mattered to my Pa. He used to say that no matter how little we had, there was a world of

"You're flying in the face of scientific fact. There are atmospheric rays which control bodily motions. If a person containing negative hexing qualities gets between you and them rays, he creates a static which jars any successful motion into an unsuccessful motion."

folks who had less. And he never got away from really doing what he talked about.

Now, let me clear up an item that might have you confused. In Fife Rule 3, I told you never to *lend* any money. Well, that rule still holds. If you come upon somebody who truly needs money, then give it. Don't lend it. You see, the feelings between lending and giving are all different. When you lend you don't solve folks' problems. You usually just delay them. When you give, you can really help. And it feels a lot better, too.

Another point I'd like to make is that giving doesn't always mean money. Milking a sick neighbor's cow, taking in a crop for another or coaching your young 'un's football team are all ways of giving, too. Whatever you decide to do, though, do it happily. It yields return sevenfold, according to the Good Book. And I believe it. So'd my Pa.

To Sum It All Up . . .

In closing let me say this: These Fife Family Rules of Finance are easy to understand but, for some reason, not quite so easy to follow. If you do follow them, although you may not get rich, you may find that you get to sleep a little quicker when you lay

down at night. And a good night's rest is worth a
whole lot. Isn't it?

**"We're just plain,
simple men
fighting organized
crime with raw
courage—strong,
determined,
rugged and
fearless."**

"I was born to sing."

10

Friendship

Show me a neighbor who'll help unclog your septic system and I'll show you a friend . . .

No book I could write would be complete without me talking about friendship. I've been blessed with friends the likes of which no man has ever had. They're the greatest part of my life, and I'm thankful.

Andy Taylor taught me about friendship. As a boys growing up in Mayberry, I considered myself about the luckiest kid in the world because Andy and me were friends. Many a day was spent with us fishing and playing ball and carrying on. He was the kind of friend who always picked me first in softball games, even though I wasn't the best player. When he had an extra dime, it was me he treated to a malt. He even did the three-legged race with me every year at the All Soul's Church annual bazaar

"Opie, let me tell you something about the newspaper business. Karen Folkers might be hot copy in the fifth grade, but uptown she don't mean a thing."

(even though we came in last nearly every year).

Andy and me have been friends since we were kids, all right. We've been through the good and the bad. I stood up for the boy when he got married. He asked

The role of godfather requires that I take an active interest in Opie's upbringing.

me to be Opie's godfather and I, of course, was proud to oblige. When the Deputy job came up, Andy interviewed me and chose the most-qualified candidate — me.

For my part, I kind'a watch over the boy. He sometimes just doesn't have the big picture, if ya' know what I mean. Like with girls. He's a good-looking-enough fella who's bright and has a pretty good personality. But for the life of me, if ol' Barn didn't take him under my wing and look out for him, he'd probably just sit home and sulk. It takes somebody like me with a little spirit to get him out of his shell. So I guess you could say that Andy's

"It's funny. Cousin Virgil's clumsy and awkward. Look at me, I'm completely coordinated, keen, sharp and alert."

and my friendship is symbonetic in that each one of us is better off because of the other.

Old Friends

For whatever reason, Andy and me have stayed friends for all of these years. And I know for sure that old friends are the best friends. As you get older you come to appreciate the times when you can sit around and talk about old times. Like talking with Andy about our days as Boy Scouts. Or like talking about kids we grew up with or about our early business ventures in door-to-door sales.

"I ain't got time to stand around here and discuss trivial trivialities."

Like talking about how they're building the new schoolhouse in the old field where Johnny broke his leg twenty-five years ago playing touch football. Or figuring out if the new Preacher's wife is the niece of your fourth-grade teacher. You can just hear the conversation as me and Andy sit in the squad car watching folks do their shopping on a Tuesday morning:

Andy: Hey, Barn, ain't that new Preacher's wife kin to Miss Moran?

Me: You mean the Moran that used to teach fourth grade?

Andy: Yeah.

Me: She favors the Morans.

Andy: Yep, she's got the same crooked nose.

Me: Miss Moran's nose wasn't always crooked.

Andy: Is that a fact?

Me: No siree. Don't you remember, Ange? Miss Moran's nose was straight 'til she had that terrible accident.

Andy: What terrible accident was that?

Me: Well , Andy, don't tell me that you've forgotten the ice storm of '46 — Asa's bum hip?

Andy: What about it?

Me: Well, Andy, you remember.

Andy: No, I don't.

Me: It's a sad thing when your memory starts to go.

Andy: My memory is fine. What happened to Asa and what's that got to do with Miss Moran's nose?

"You never heard of Jim Lindsey's big hit 'Rock and Roll Rosie from Raleigh'?"

Me: Well, it's got everything in the world to do with it.

Andy: What?

Me: You remember. Asa was walking home from his job at the barrel factory after the ice storm when he met up with Miss Moran taking her groceries home. Asa offered to carry them for her so she wouldn't fall on the ice with her arms full. Well, just when Asa reaches to take the bags off her hands, his feet slip out from under him and he starts to fall. The bags went flying and a jar of pickles busts Miss Moran's nose. That's how it got crooked.

Andy: Well, I'll be dogged.

Me: Even without the nose she looks like a Moran.

Andy: Could be . . .

I reckon that being able to talk of old times makes a friendship richer than almost anything else.

"My column in the school paper 'Pickups and Splashes from Floor and Pool' was controversial. It was way ahead of its time."

Reunions

A good time for reminiscing about the old times is reunions. In Mayberry the annual reunion of graduates of Mayberry Union High (the old Orange and Blue) is a real fine way to rekindle old friendships. It's always one of the high points of the year, especially when the graduates of the Class of '45 get back together. What a wild lot they are!

Of course, reunions can have their drawbacks like anything else. Like seeing folks like Jack Egbert, who once blackballed me when I was trying to join the Philomathian Literary Society in high school. There's one fella that I haven't missed a bit. He

On the Mayberry social scale, Mayberry Union High Reunions are numero uno.

probably went off and married some dull girl and founded the Philomathian Society of High Point. Serves him right. He can paste up scrapbooks the rest of his life as far as I'm concerned. He can have his old Society. It was a stupid waste of time anyhow.

Forgiveness — *The Key to Friendship*

There are times when misunderstandings can call a halt to even the best friendships. They'll happen. They're just a fact of life. It's how ya' handle them that makes the difference.

"I come before you a humble man, full of humbleness and humility."

Many folks choose to carry a grudge through their lives for events that are long past. But take us Fifes, on the other hand. We have always been forgiving. It's just our nature. Daddy Fife had a saying:

Forgive, forgive, forgive . . . and let folks live, live, live.

There hasn't been a Fife born who could find it in his heart to carry a grudge. Like water off a duck's back flow the wrongs that have been done to us Fifes over the years. And there have been many, I'll assure you of that. But do we hold on to them? No. Never. Not a Fife. And if anybody were ever justified in carrying a grudge, it would be us, ya' know. You betcha'. We have every reason in the world to be bitter. Like the time . . .

Clubs and Organizations

Friendships built around common interests are some of the best. Things like the Mayberry Garden Club, the Masons and the Mayberry Town Choir. As you know, it's through one of these groups that Wally came to hire Gomer to work for him.

Years ago Wally was singing first tenor (There were only two tenors, so one of them sang first tenor and one second.) for John Masters in the choir. It happened that they were practicing for the Fourth of July concert when Gilly Parker's cousin talked him into playing poker and skipping rehearsal. Since Gilly was the only other tenor except for Wally, this left John Masters, the choir and especially Wally in a terrible fix.

Well, Andy had heard Gomer sing while he was working on a car and invited him to choir practice. Luckily for Wally, Gomer showed up and the Independence Day concert went on without a hitch. Shortly thereafter, Wally hired Gomer on at the filling station. They've been friends ever since (for the most part).

(As a man of trained voice, it's my opinion that Gomer has a rough, but trainable, voice. It sure needs a lot of work, though. What folks just don't under-

"Raleigh is where I really belong . . . Barney Fife in the Asphalt Jungle."

stand is that good singing takes a load of training. Take me, for instance. It's taken years of training under Eleanora Poultice for me to refine the gift of voice that I was given. But I was willing to pay the price. The price of stardom is work, work, work. Goes to show ya' — put talent and hard work and Eleanora Poultice in a bag and shake it up — and what do ya' get? A crooner, that's what. Frank Sinatra . . . Ted Weems . . . Barney Fife. Crooners, every one of us!)

"Leonard Blush's rise to stardom was very meteoric."

The Regal Order of the Golden Door to Good Fellowship is one other club that I'll mention because it is solely dedicated to friendship I've never seen a better place for folks to get together, share a root beer, play some checkers and get to know each other. It's done a lot of good through the years and I think there ought to be more groups just like it.

Floyd's Barber Shop

Notwithstanding any of the above, the finest place for passing the time with your friends in Mayberry is Floyd's Barber Shop. Many's the problem that's been solved around that checker table. I don't know what we would do if we couldn't meet at Floyd's. And as you'll recall, that almost happened once when Howard Sprague bought the shop and tried to raise Floyd's rent. Fortunately, they compromised or else we would've just had to say *adios* to the number one social spot in Mayberry.

Sometimes if a man can talk through his problems with a couple of friends it all of a sudden makes sense. You can say all you want about counselors and the such, but to get to the root of things, go get a haircut. Plain and simple, it's therapeutic.

Floyd's is really more than a barber shop, though. It's kind'a like a home base in this rush-

"Incarcerated means being put into prison. Inarculated is a shot you get from your doctor."

The wit and wisdom of Mayberry is shared daily at Floyd's.

It never hurts to have your Pa and your best fishing buddy be the same man.

and-hurry world of ours. Just like Reverend Breen from New York said, we all need a place to slow down and appreciate life. It's like a little island of calm in the fast-paced, exciting world that we call Mayberry.

"You're funny, all right. You're a scream. You ought to get a job on one of them excursion boats."

Running Into Trouble

Let's face it — sometimes even the best friendships run into trouble of one kind or another. Every now and again friends have a falling-out. That's just natural. Really good friends know that such things happen and shouldn't be taken too seriously. Take Andy and me, for instance. It happens now and again that one of us will temporarily overstep the bounds of our friendship. Things can get pretty sticky when that happens.

Ya' see, sometimes Andy forgets just how sensitive us Fifes are. My mother is sensitive and so was her mother. It just runs in my mother's side of the family.   I can take good-natured ribbing as good as the next guy because I was blessed with a good sense of humor, which is another Fife trait. That's two traits of us Fifes — great sense of humor, but real sensitive. Enjoy a good laugh, but still sensitive.

"My name is F-I-F-E; for the third time you've printed F-I-K-E. You're a newspaper man, you'd think you could spell."

Overdoing It

One thing I can't stand, though, is Andy — or anyone else, for that matter — overdoing it. Like when Andy ribs me about having a clock in my stomach. He just doesn't take seriously the needs of a high-strung man like

"You're funny, you know that? You know you're as funny as a crutch."

me when it comes to eating on time. Well, it's one thing kidding with me about the clock in *my* stomach, but it's another thing entirely when he jokes about my Ma having a clock in her stomach. Sure, she likes to eat on time like any other healthy person, but that doesn't give Andy call to kid about her. That's just plain and simple a case of overdoing it. Talking about my Ma and all — and after my Ma treated Andy like a son. He sure has his nerve!

Now, on those occasions when Andy overdoes it, the best thing for me to do is just to nip it. Nip it in the bud! Right then and there. Nip it! Of course, we all know that Andy's got good intentions, but when he gets carried away he just needs to be reminded of my nature. The fact is, my nature is one thing Andy should understand. I understand his nature. But then again I do a lot of reading of psychological magazines like *True Blue Detective*. He really should read more on psychological matters. Then he'd see the world more clearly — more like I do. Could you imagine what Mayberry would be like if the Sheriff were as well versed in psychology as I am? But I guess Andy just ain't as interested in probing the subconscious as I am. Too bad. He could really learn a lot.

"Folks in Mayberry ain't got a better friend than Andy Taylor. If you tried to take him out of office . . . then you'd have a riot."

Special Friendships

There are some types of friendships that are unique. These are the friendships between folks that are related. I've always figured that because we are free to choose our friends, we should be able to get along with them, but that ain't true of relatives. One day you're an only child and the next day you've got a brother or a sister. There was nothing you could have done about it, even had you been asked (which, of course, you weren't).

As we all know, family members are supposed to get along just because they're family members. As best as I can see, this just doesn't carry water. It's a wonderful thing for families to be close-knit, but it never surprises me when I see brothers and sisters that ain't. All that business of sharing at a young age sometimes festers into a real problem later on. For this reason, I'm always thrilled to see family members who, in addition to being related, are also friends.

Opie and Andy are as close as a boy and his Pa can be. But part of the reason for that closeness is the way Andy has set himself up as not only the boy's father but also a friend. When you can be both family and friend you've got the best of both worlds. And that's just what Andy and his boy have got going for them.

But being a friend to a little boy doesn't mean being an easy touch. Many's the time when Andy has to do something firm-handed to keep Ope on the straight and narrow. What I've noticed, though, is that whenever Andy uses that firm hand, it's wrapped real thick with love. They have a wonder-

ful thing — a friendship between a boy and his Pa.
Maybe one day the time'll be right and I'll have
myself a little son. I sure do dream of having a friend
like that some day . . . .

. . . *that Andy's a lucky fella.*

"I don't chew my cabbage twice."

11

Childhood and Growing Up

Even the mighty oak is obliged to a
tiny acorn . . .

I think that growing up in Mayberry was about the luckiest thing that ever happened to me. I've heard about bright lights and big cities. I've been around. I've heard all about New York and Gay Paree. But I don't think they have much over Mayberry. Sure, they may have more excitement, but who needs that? We have all the excitement we need right here. And even if we didn't, we have lots of things a lot more important than excitement — things like good friends and healthy air and clean streets. Nope, I wouldn't have wanted to be raised anywhere else — not by a long shot.

"The practice of Judo will allow one to cultivate courage and endure hardship."

Mayberry Is Family

Ya' see, the folks of Mayberry are family. Not that we're all related, though many of us are (like me and cousin Andy). But when you're raised in a family-like setting, it's a safe, slow process. Being a young boy in Mayberry teaches kids about life just like New York does, but in a kinda slow and gentle way.

Take, for example, when a new baby's born in Mayberry. It's not just something that happens a hundred times a day like in a big city hospital. No siree. It's a real important thing and everybody is pulling for that young 'un even before he's born. Like the time Mrs. Morgan was expecting. Jess, her husband, came down with the flu right during the harvest and couldn't even get out'a bed. There was Mrs. Morgan out trying to take in the crops all by herself. And being only weeks away from delivering their baby!

As luck would have it, Wally was driving in from Winston-Salem (He'd been visiting his sister, Bertha, the one who was Miss Okra last year.) when he saw Mrs. Morgan out working in the field. It wasn't two hours before Emmett had closed down his Fixit Shop and taken ten other fellas out to Jess's place to take in the crop. It took 'em two full days, but

> "Asa, let me show you what a bullet should look like. Now this is bullet maintenance."

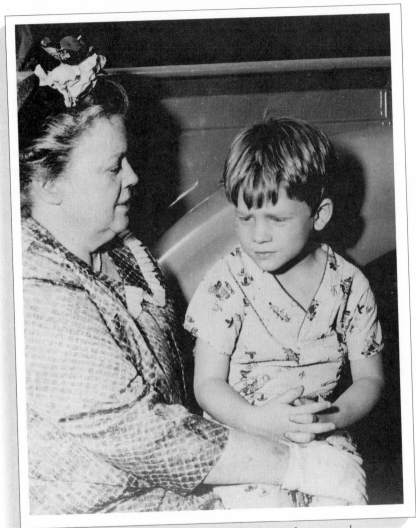

Aunt Bee is a special woman, as Opie found out early on . . . and her lap is a perfect fit.

they got it in before it was too late. Doc Bennett said that a woman in her condition doing such work would'a surely made the baby come early. Instead, Mrs. Morgan had a beautiful baby girl who was as healthy as a horse and as pretty as a peacock.

But that's just the way it is in Mayberry. Folks take care of folks. Always has been that way, always will be.

"A wink is as good as a knod to a blind mule."

Right and Wrong

Now, as a young 'un grows up in Mayberry he learns real quick the difference between right and wrong. I know that in other places folks are encouraged to do whatever makes them feel good, but in Mayberry we have a little more clear set of rules. We've found that young 'uns do best when we keep things real simple. Like explaining why it's good to tell the truth and why it isn't good to steal. The last thing they need to hear is that maybe it's OK to do this or that, but it depends on the situation. That doesn't answer questions. Does nothing but confuse the young 'un. Nope, in Mayberry, we say right is right and wrong is wrong. Period.

Now, once a kid learns the basic rules he can learn that the world isn't black and white. When he's older he can figure out the gray areas. But you've got to put down the basics first, before complicating the situation with all the exceptions.

Sometimes, of course, it's a little tough to teach the exceptions. Boy, I remember Andy had a tough time explaining to Opie why it was OK to throw out Aunt Bee's pickles. Those darned pickles. Kerosene cucumbers is what they were! I remember thinking that life just wasn't worth living with eight quarts of those pickles in the future. Nonetheless, Andy sure had trouble convincing Opie that throwing them out and replacing them with store pickles wasn't dishonest — it was just a small trick to save Aunt Bee's feelings. I don't know if Opie ever understood, but, as you know, we ended up eating those awful cucumbers anyway. I still think of 'em every time a truck goes by. Ugh.

> **"You're real funny, you are. It's too bad you're not twins. You could be the Katzenjammer Kids."**

The Bible Belt

The first lesson a young 'un learns in Mayberry is that he's gonna be raised according to the rules of the Bible Belt. That rule was explained to me real early — Mother Fife had a Bible in her left hand and a belt in the right one. You pretty much got to choose, but it was real clear that if you didn't

In Mayberry, everybody cares for everybody else . . . from the oldest to the youngest.

There's nothing better for a young 'un than time spent with his Pa.

choose the path of the Bible, you got the belt.

Now, I'm sure many folks would say that this system doesn't work and makes kids grow up confused. But it occurs to me that this way worked for a couple of thousand years before anybody ever heard of a fella named Sigmund Frude. And if ya' ask me it worked a lot better.

A Good Example

"This is just the kind of case that would be good for us. It would keep our instincts honed up razor sharp."

There's a right way and there's a wrong way. And you could learn the right one just by watching the good citizens of Mayberry. I already told ya' about Jess and Mrs. Morgan. But that's just one example. Why, every day the young 'uns are taught by the example of their elders. Like the time a man came visiting from England. He had saved every bit of his money for years to take a bicycle tour of America. Merriweather was his name, yeah, Malcolm Merriweather from Heckmondwyke, England. Well, anyway, he came riding into town and got himself into a terrible wreck. (I think it was the roads. I hear they drive on the wrong side of the roads over in England. I figure that he just got confused. That happens a lot to those folks from across the big water. At least that's what Andy told me to write in the report that we sent to Raleigh.)

That boy has fine taste in teachers. So does his Pa!

Anyway, by the time Wally and Gomer look over the damage, it comes to more money than the foreigner had. So, what happens to this fella who's half-way around the world from home? Jail? Sell his bicycle to pay the difference? No way. Next thing you know, Andy's got him doing chores and fixing up things at his house and the such. Then

"It's from little misdemeanors that major felonies grow."

Aunt Bee leaves and Mr. Merriweather takes up housekeeping to work off his debt.

So let me ask you: If you were a kid and you watched this all happen, would you learn any lessons about life? And the young 'uns sure enough notice how grown-ups handle situations like this. In Mayberry that's how young 'uns see the grown-ups behave. They think that's the way it's *supposed* to be. Which, of course, it is.

Now, if you're a young 'un like Opie or Leon or Johnny Paul Jason and you see a stranger treated like this, what's it teach you? I'll tell you what it teaches 'em. It teaches 'em more than all of the lectures in the world. I guess you could say that my advice is to spend less time telling kids what to do and take a lot more time showing 'em. In Mayberry, things are a little slower, and there's still time for the little things — like setting a good example.

> "The first sign that a youngster is going bad, you got to nip it in the bud. Don't mollycoddle him."

The Tough Parts of Growing Up

Now, in some ways Mayberry is no different than any other place on earth. It has its troubles and its worries. Folks get sick in Mayberry. Folks can't pay their bills in Mayberry. There's sadness and loneliness in Mayberry. There's dishonesty and crime, too. But bigger than any of these problems are the hearts of the citizens of Mayberry. The difference is how folks deal with troubles in a small town. If one fella has a problem, everybody has a problem. And more often than not, with everybody carrying part of the load, we work through our problems lickety-split. And as much as anything else, knowing that sure makes growing up a whole lot easier.

I guess what I'm saying is that growing up in Mayberry is a twenty-year lesson that's taught day by day by good people who care to see that a youngster gets off to a good start. I just don't know how growing up can get any better than that.

> **"That badge means something. Don't any of you disgrace it. If there's trouble, I want no molly coddling."**

12

I Gotta Run, But...

Eleven o'clock and all is well . . .

Well, I guess it's about time to head out and lock 'er up for the night. It must be close to eleven. Nobody'll be out tonight. It's just one of those cool North Carolina nights when the crickets chirp and the fireflies blink and the cool breeze puts a little tingle in your skin. Nobody'll be out tonight, even though it's a beautiful night for wandering.

This is one of the parts of the job of being Deputy that I like the best. You know why? The reason I like this part so much is because it just makes me so proud.

"You better gird your loins, Buster, because you've got a fight on your hands."

All over town folks have turned in knowing that they'll get a good night's rest. Not a one of 'em is worried that lurking in the night is something that they should fear. They've laid their heads down trusting that everything will be all right, at least for another night.

Mothers have tucked their babies down in the soft covers and fathers have turned off the lights and checked the stove. They've closed up their homes to end another day without so much as a thought that there may be danger out there, waiting, patiently, to do them harm.

Storekeepers have pulled down their shades and locked their doors, closing inside their dreams and wares. Never do they think that their treasures may be in danger. And do you know why all of these nice things happen every night in Mayberry? Do ya'? It's because . . .

"The most relaxing, peaceful place I know is Floyd Lawson's barber shop."

~~~~~~~~~~~~~

Barney Fife's on duty, and all's right with the world.

~~~~~~~~~~~~~